Connecticut Signer: William Williams

Connecticut Signer: William Williams

By BRUCE P. STARK

Guilford, Connecticut

Published by Globe Pequot
An imprint of The Rowman & Littlefield Publishing Group, Inc.
4501 Forbes Boulevard, Suite 200, Lanham, Maryland 20706
www.rowman.com

Unit A, Whitacre Mews, 26-34 Stannary Street, London SE11 4AB

Distributed by NATIONAL BOOK NETWORK

Copyright © 1975 by The American Revolution Bicentennial Commission of Connecticut
A Publication of The American Revolution Bicentennial Commission of Connecticut
First Globe Pequot paperback edition 2017

British Library Cataloguing in Publication Information Available

Library of Congress Cataloging-in-Publication Data
The paperback edition of this book was previously cataloged by the Library of Congress as follows:

ISBN: 87106-061-2
Library of Congress Catalog Card Number: 75-27801

ISBN 978-0-87106-061-7 (paper : alk. paper)
ISBN 978-1-49303-310-2 (electronic)

∞™ The paper used in this publication meets the minimum requirements of American National Standard for Information Sciences—Permanence of Paper for Printed Library Materials, ANSI/ NISO Z39.48-1992.

Printed in the United States of America

Contents

A Lebanon Boyhood and Youth

W ILLIAM WILLIAMS, fourth son of the Reverend Solomon and Mary Porter Williams, was born on March 18, 1730/31, in Lebanon, Connecticut, an eastern, interior farm community. William, or Bille as he was called as a youth, had three older brothers who lived to adulthood, one younger brother, and three younger sisters. His father, Solomon Williams (1700-1776), pastor of the First Church in Lebanon between 1722 and 1776, was the son of the Reverend William Williams (1665-1741) of Hatfield, Massachusetts, by his second wife, Christian, daughter of the Reverend Solomon Stoddard of Northampton.[1] Solomon received an A.B. from Harvard in 1719 and accepted the unanimous call to the pulpit in Lebanon on February 27, 1721/22. His ordination took place on December 5, and one and a half months later he married Mary Porter of Hadley, Massachusetts. A popular preacher and a noted scholar, he was the leading figure in the founding and promotion of Lebanon's Philogrammatician Library in 1739, instrumental in establishing Lebanon's grammar school, an enthusiastic supporter of Eleazar Wheelock's Indian Charity School, and a member of the Corporation of Yale College. He earned a reputation as one of the leading divines in the colony and was an ardent supporter of the Great Awakening.[2] Solomon Williams had a deep and pervasive influence on the life and career of his most famous son, for from his father, William Williams inherited a deep respect for learning, an abiding religious faith, and New Light political sentiments.

The Lebanon of Williams' youth was a rapidly-growing and expanding agricultural community. The town encompassed eighty square miles and consisted of part of a large area in northeastern Connecticut that was opened for settlement after King Philip's War. Settlement began in 1695, and the area was named Lebanon in 1697 by the Reverend James Fitch, because a swamp of cedars reminded him of the Biblical cedars of Lebanon. The First Church was organized on November 27, 1700, under the pastoral care of the Reverend Joseph Parsons. An indication of the rapid growth and geographical expansion of population is seen in the creation of new parishes. Crank Society, in the northern portion of town, was organized in 1715, and Goshen, in the western section, in 1729. The number of trainbands also increased with the population. Lebanon's first militia company was formed in 1702. At the time of William Williams' birth, the town contained four trainbands, and by the outbreak of the Revolution the town counted six. The years between 1725 and 1740 marked the period of greatest economic growth in Lebanon. The list of polls and rateable estates totalled £12,404 in 1725, and had leaped to £31,709 by 1740. In 1705, the first year the townspeople were obliged to pay colony taxes, the list totalled just £3,736, ranking the town twenty-third of thirty-three towns taxed. The grand list for 1725 ranked Lebanon nineteenth of forty-three towns, while the list for 1740 placed the town the sixth highest in the colony. By 1755, the date of Connecticut's first official census, Lebanon's grand list had only increased to £38,214, at which time the town counted 3,171 whites and 103 blacks. Lebanon's population had doubled since William Williams' birth, and it ranked as one of the wealthiest and most populous towns in Connecticut. According to the 1756 census, Lebanon ranked ninth of seventy-three towns in population. The 1774 census showed that the town had 3,841 whites, ninety-eight Negroes and twenty-one Indians. The town was then fourteenth of seventy-six in population, and the town's list was eleventh highest in the colony.[8]

Lebanon was a subsistence-agricultural community, and was thus similar to most other Connecticut towns. Subsistence societies were middle-class and small-farm in character, having few wealthy citizens and no large class of landless laborers. Fifteen miles of poor roads separated the town from the nearest seaport, thus the expense of transporting such agricultural surpluses that were produced was high, and farmers could compete normally only in local markets. Primitive agricultural methods, combined with overintensive use of inadequate soil, made farming largely unremunerative.[4] In 1800, Elkanah Tisdale, a prominent Lebanon lawyer, described the character of the land in a piece written for the Connecticut Academy of Arts and Sciences:

> The Town has in it many hills or large swells of land, but few of them steep, generally Stoney & hard to till, with a bed of gravel about a foot & half below the Surface . . . . Between the hills are generally found runs of water bordered by meadow or swamp ground with some tracts of level, sandy thin soiled land, excellent for corn if sufficiently Manured, otherwise not very productive.

Corn, rye, and wheat were the principal grain crops, although some oats and buckwheat were also grown. Farmers also produced pork, beef, and cheese. Few farms were rented, and Tisdale noted further that "perhaps no Town can be found where the Lands are more equally distributed."[5] Professionals were few in number. At the time of William Williams' birth, Lebanon counted three ministers, one doctor, and one lawyer. The leading merchant was Joseph Trumbull, father of the Revolutionary War Governor.[6]

The frontier era in Lebanon ended about the time of Williams' birth, for in 1730, the town proprietors made the final division of land. Population continued to expand rapidly throughout the years of Williams' youth, but slowed markedly by the 1750s.[7] With more than fifty persons per square mile, Lebanon was overpopulated. Poor soil and primitive agricultural methods led to rapid soil exhaustion, and the younger generation was forced to seek its fortune elsewhere. One quarter of males taxed in 1761 had departed by the time of the Revolution. A handful of persons emigrated to Nova Scotia and to the Susquehannnah Territory in Pennsylvania, but far larger numbers moved to western Massachusetts, present Vermont, and New Hampshire. Since Lebanon was an isolated, subsistence-agricultural community, middle-class living standards could only be maintained if large numbers departed.[8]

Four separate branches of the Williams family had settled in Lebanon in the first quarter of the eighteenth century, three descended from Robert Williams (1607-1693) of Roxbury, Massachusetts, and the fourth from Nicholas (1616-1692) of Roxbury, the younger brother of Robert. The line of Robert Williams was numerous and distinguished, particularly in the Congregationalist ministry. Solomon's father, the Reverend William Williams of Hatfield, and John Williams (1664-1729), minister at Deerfield, were two of the most distinguished.[9] The eldest son of John, Eleazar Williams, was graduated from Harvard College and served as the first minister in Mansfield, Connecticut, from 1710 until 1742. The Reverend Eleazar Williams was well-liked by his parishioners. He delivered the election sermon in 1723. A friend of revived religion, he died on September 21, 1742, and Solomon Williams preached his funeral sermon. Another son, Stephen (1693-1782), served in the ministry in Long Meadow, Massachusetts. Three of Stephen's sons, Stephen (1722-1795), Warham (1726-1788), and Nathan (1734-1829), were also ministers. All were graduated from Yale and labored in Connecticut—at Woodstock, Northford Parish in Branford, and Tolland. Eleazar and Stephen Williams were Solomon's second cousins.[10] Another second cousin, Ebenezer Williams (1690-1753), was ordained in October, 1715, as the first minister in Pomfret. Ebenezer enjoyed great influence among the clergy and served as trustee of Yale College. Solomon Williams also delivered his funeral sermon. A younger brother, William (1698-1766), also lived in Pomfret, and members of this branch of the family were counted among the political leaders of that community.[11] Solomon's half-brother, Elisha (1694-1755), was Rector of Yale College between 1725 and 1739. A resident of Wethersfield, he also served as Clerk of the Assembly, Speaker of the House, and Judge of the Superior Court. Two uncles, John (1667-1702) and Eleazar (1669-1725), moved to Stonington. Eleazar resided in Lebanon from 1708 until 1715, and was the first Williams to dwell there. He was elected Selectman in December, 1711, but removed to Stonington in 1715.[12]

The first Williams to settle in town permanently was Parke Wiliams (1677-1757) of Roxbury, younger brother of the Reverend John

Williams of Deerfield. Parke arrived in mid-1711 and was admitted an inhabitant in December. He fathered two sons, Samuel (1699-1775) and John (1706-1774), Harvard, 1725, who were Solomon Williams' second cousins. Parke became a freeman but never filled any important offices. Samuel held four minor town positions and served in twenty-four parish offices. The townspeople elected John Williams to the legislature three times and also chose him Deacon of the First Church. In 1744, however, he removed to newly-settled Sharon in Litchfield County. He quickly became the most important figure in his community. He served the town as Representative and Justice of the Peace. He was chosen Judge of the Court of Probate for the Sharon district, was chosen Judge of the County Court in October, 1754, and in 1767 was made Lieutenant Colonel of the Fourteenth Militia Regiment.[13]

Daniel Williams (1683-1737) of Killingworth, grandson of Nicholas, removed to Lebanon in October, 1711. This branch of the family was numerous but not distinguished. Daniel had four sons, Daniel, Isaiah, Samuel, and Israel. They were third cousins of Solomon Williams.[14] Ebenezer Williams (1691-1740), a first cousin, moved to Lebanon in 1718. Ebenezer twice served as Selectman and also as militia officer. Ebenezer had three sons who were contemporaries of William Williams. Jonathan (1722-1805) held twenty-one town and four society offices, and, in addition, served ten times as Moderator of the Goshen Society meetings. Vetch (1727-1804) served as militia officer, was chosen Selectman for fourteen years, and twice represented Lebanon in the legislature. Isaac (1729-1814) served one term as Selectman in 1786.[15] In addition to Lebanon, Williams' lived in the Wethersfield, Sharon, Mansfield, Pomfret, Stonington, and Killingworth areas. Almost invariably, several members of the family served in the legislature at the same time. In May, 1757, the first occasion William Williams was present, four others were Deputies—Elisha Williams, Jr., of Wethersfield, son of the Rector, Ebenezer Williams of Pomfret, John Williams of Sharon, and John Williams of Stonington.[16]

Ecclesiastically, the Williams family ranked among the first families in Connecticut. Solomon Williams, Elisha Williams, Eleazar Williams of Mansfield, Ebenezer Williams of Pomfret, Warham Williams of Branford, and Eliphalet Williams of East Hartford, Solomon's eldest surviving son, marked the family both by numbers and influence as perhaps the outstanding clerical family in the colony.[17] Politically, only Rector Elisha Williams earned a colony-wide reputation prior to the appearance of William Williams. John Williams of Sharon, Ebenezer and Thomas Williams of Pomfret, and William and John Williams of Stonington earned significant reputations in their own localities, but none filled such important positions as Clerk, Speaker, or Judge of the Superior Court as did Elisha Williams.[18] In the political sphere, the Williams clan could be counted among the second-rank, ruling families of Connecticut, locally important, but not producing Governors and Assistants like the Talcotts, Pitkins, Wolcotts, and Huntingtons.

When William Williams launched his political career, he possessed important assets. Except for the Clark family, more Williams' lived in Lebanon than any other family. His father was liked and respected by his parishioners, and he was one of the best-known divines in the colony. Uncle Elisha had a colony-wide reputation earned as Rector of Yale, Speaker, and Judge. These connections, in an age of deference, must be weighed as impressive political assets. The closeness of the Williams and Trumbull families also boosted the career of young William Williams. Such factors, together with his own obvious merits, opened the way to a successful political career.

The eldest son of Solomon Williams was Solomon (1725-1743). He died in Lebanon on October 24, 1743, less than two months after his graduation from Yale.[19] Eliphalet Williams (1727-1803) was also graduated from Yale in 1743. He studied theology with his father, and on March 30, 1748, was ordained pastor of the church in East Hartford. Three years later, Eliphalet married Mary Williams, daughter of Rector Elisha. Replacing his father, he served as Fellow of Yale College from 1769 to 1801, and in appreciation Yale granted him a degree of Doctor of Divinity in 1782. Like other members of the family, he enthusiastically supported the Patriot cause.[20] Ezekiel (1729-1818), the only son not to receive a college education, moved to Wethersfield and, in 1760, married a second cousin, Prudence Stoddard of Northampton. In February, 1767, he was appointed Sheriff of Hartford County, a position he held until 1789. He, too, ardently supported the American cause. Fellow townsmen Silas Deane condescendingly wrote about his enthusiasm in April 1774:

> This town met on Thursday, this week; they are spirited. But Sheriff Williams, in his boiling zeal, has almost preached them to death; he neglects serving writs or levying executions, and is now so hoarse that he can only whisper, but his desire of communicating is no way abated, which, were the subject less interesting than it is, would render him a diverting figure.

Once fighting broke out, Ezekiel was appointed to the Committee of the Pay Table, and in May, 1777, he was chosen a Commissary of Prisoners. He retained both positions throughout the war.[21] Mary Williams (1733-1794) in 1768 married the Reverend Richard Salter, pastor of the First Church in Mansfield from 1744 to 1787. Thomas (1735-1819) was graduated from Yale in 1756 and was a practicing physician in Lebanon. Christian married John Salter of Mansfield, a prominent citizen of that town who served as Representative and Justice of the Peace. The youngest daughter, Eunice (1745-1831), married the Reverend Timothy Stone of Goshen Parish in Lebanon.[22]

William Williams spent his childhood in a rapidly-growing agricultural community in the midst of a large and affectionate family. The atmosphere was both religious and learned. Bille had not reached his eighth birthday, when the Philogrammatician Library was founded. Five local ministers and seven laymen from Lebanon covenanted together with Solomon Williams on January 4, 1738/39, to form the library, the first in Windham County and only the fourth in the colony. The participants agreed to furnish £50 "Current money" to Solomon Williams "to purchase and buy a Library of. . . useful and profitable books." Williams ordered books from Boston, and three extant book lists show that the library contained 103 volumes. A majority were religious in nature, but the library also included seventeen law books, eight medical books, sixteen histories and encyclopedias, and one volume on science. The library was located in the First Society, probably at the home of Solomon Williams, and thus the Williams children had easy access to it.[23]

The Great Awakening burst on the Connecticut scene a year and a half later, spawned by an electrifying young Anglican preacher, George Whitefield. New England divines, none more ardently than Solomon Williams, had long prayed for and awaited anxiously for spiritual renewal, and the Awakening had an unprecedented and traumatic effect on the spiritual and political consciousness of Connecticut. The entire colony was touched by the revival, but no area more than in Windham and New London Counties. Enthusiasm for the revival was due in large measure to the social and political configuration of the region—rapid growth and turmoil over land titles, religion, currency, and local matters. These tensions weakened the social structure, a fabric already impaired by rapid economic expansion, and they served to alienate the population from their natural social and religious leaders.[24] But the revival also had a momentous impact in eastern Connecticut because the leading ministers ardently supported awakened religion. Among the leaders of the revival in northeastern Connecticut were Joseph Meacham of Coventry, Eleazar Williams of Mansfield, Benjamin Pomeroy of Hebron, Eleazar Wheelock of Lebanon Crank, and Solomon Williams. Aiming to cleanse the churches from a century's growth of impurities, the Great Awakening produced an astounding increase in the number of church admissions. In 1741, ninety-five persons joined the First Church in full communion, five times the average for a normal year. Another fifty-two were admitted the next year. Sixty-six admissions were recorded for the Goshen Church, an impressive total, since the population of Goshen Society was much smaller than that of the First Society, and especially since the minister, Jacob Eliot, did not support the revival. The revival descended upon Lebanon in July, 1741. Jacob Eliot noted in his diary on July 9, that "Mr. Williams preached his lecture, Is[aiah] 33:13-14. A very awakening sermon, a great groang & cryg out." During July, forty-two persons joined the church in full communion.[25]

Solomon Williams was a moderate New Light. He believed that the revival was evidence of God's work, but he opposed the emotional excesses that ultimately alienated a majority of the standing political and ecclesiastical order. Trances and visions could not be depended upon, said Williams, for they could come from either Heaven or Hell. True Christians should not depend on visions as a mark of God's grace, for man should "have no Christ but what is Reveal'd in the Bible," and man should remember that "Prayer is one of the chief Means and Instruments of Communion with God." Persons living without prayer lived without God. On the other hand, Williams did not believe that God dealt with man by filling him "with a Slavish fear and dread of him." Some ardent souls even considered Pastor Williams an Arminian. He accepted all persons who offered themselves for the communion, provided they had a basic knowledge of religion and were free from scandal. He did not believe that God delighted in man's miseries, and he did not hold that premonitions were necessarily revelations.[26] New Lights represented an ecclesiastical minority in Connecticut after 1740, and, due to the intimate connection between church and state, religious controversies inevitably became political controversies. William Williams did not join his father's church until 1757, but the revival had an overwhelming effect on the boy. It could not help but heighten his religious sensibilities, and, when he entered politics, he aligned himself with the New Light party.

Young Williams prepared for college by studying with his father, and probably by attending Lebanon's grammar school. His brothers matriculated at Yale, but William attended Harvard, his father's *alma mater*. He entered college in 1747, when he was sixteen, and held the Browne and Gibbs scholarships. Only three glimpses of him exist during his college years. Uncle Israel of Hatfield wrote to brother Solomon on November 29, 1748, that he had recently seen their children, William and John, at Cambridge.[27] "They are well, and are very desirous of coming home this Winter. I consented & proposed that they should be absent at ye Same time from College." Israel believed they should not absent themselves from college for long, and he asked Solomon's opinion on the subejct.[28]

In March, 1750, the pastor informed brother Elisha that illness had descended upon the family. On January 2, Ezekiel came down with throat distemper. Three days later, Christian contracted the same disease, and, within another week, Tommy, Moses, and Bille all became seriously ill. Moses died on January 12, but the rest survived. Bille and Christian had "pretty well Recovered," but Ezekiel and Tommy "have but just Escaped the Grave & are still in a Miserable Languishing State." The next May, shortly before graduation, Solomon informed his son that he would be "down the week before Commencement and shall bring what you expect from your Mother viz your Gown and Jacket and Shirts," and, like all good parents, he enclosed money. William received his A.B. in 1751, was granted an *ad eundem* A.B. from Yale in 1753, and an M.A. "in course" from Harvard in 1754. When he received his second degree from Harvard, Williams argued in his "disputation" that the Scripture was perfect.[29]

Williams was evidently intended for the ministry, and, after earning his A.B. he studied theology under his father. By 1756, however, he had decided to become a merchant, which, in his case, was a glorified name for shopkeeper. By Connecticut's modest standards, he did well. His chief interest, however, was politics, and, along with ambition, ability, and family connections, he brought luck to this endeavor, an important ingredient for success in any sphere. Any young man with a college degree and possessing such an eminent father could look forward to a successful political career, had he ambition and a minimal ability to win popular esteem. William Williams was only twenty-one and a half when the townspeople of Lebanon elected him Town Clerk and Town Treasurer.[30] At this infant stage of his political career, luck played a crucial role in giving Williams the first and most important step up the ladder of success. Williams attained a prestigous office that placed him at the center of town affairs, due to the premature death of the incumbent Clerk and Treasurer, Gershom Clark (1726-1752).

Clark was clearly marked for political prominence. A graduate of Yale, class of 1743, he was scion of the most numerous and distinguished family in early Lebanon. His father, Gershom Clark (1697-1747), served as militia officer, Selectman, Representative, Justice of the Peace, and Town Clerk and Treasurer. Two uncles, William and Joseph Clark, enjoyed equal prominence, while Gershom's grandfather, William Clark, Esq. (1665-1725), was the outstanding figure in Lebanon's founding generation. William Clark was one of the first three men chosen Selectman, was one of nine original members of the church, was the first person to represent Lebanon in the General Assembly, and was the first man chosen Justice of the Peace. He also captained Lebanon's trainband, served at Town Clerk, was chosen Selectman seventeen times, served as Representative nineteen times, was the first person from northeastern Connecticut to be nominated to the Upper House, and was, moreover, one of two proprietors of the huge Clark and Dewey Purchase in Lebanon, a tract of land totalling more than thirty square miles. Gershom Clark became Clerk and Treasurer upon his father's death in August, 1747. He served in that office until his own untimely demise on November 2, 1752.[31] Clearly, by lineage, education, and position, young Clark could have looked forward to a long and distinguished political career. A competitor for political advancement

14

like Gershom Clark could have delayed and perhaps ultimately frustrated Williams' political ambitions, had not death removed him from the scene.

Williams would remain Town Clerk and Treasurer for forty-four years. He became a freeman in April, 1755, and in 1759, when he was twenty-eight, he was elected Selectman for the first of twenty-seven consecutive terms. He was chosen Clerk of the First Society in 1754 and Treasurer in 1765. He retained both positions through 1774, when duties of a more pressing nature led to his resignation. The Society Meeting also frequently chose Williams to serve on the Seating Committee and the School Money Committee. The admitted inhabitants in April, 1757, chose Williams, along with respected political veteran, Colonel Joseph Fowler, to represent the town at the May session of the General Assembly. Between May, 1757, and May, 1776, when Williams was elevated to the Chamber of Assistants, he represented Lebanon in the Lower House in every session except three. By the time he had reached his thirtieth birthday, Williams was already recognized as one of the half-dozen leading figures in town, and had long since outdistanced his contemporaries. He had served as Clerk and Treasurer for nine years, was in his second term as Selectman, had, in 1759, been chosen Justice of the Peace, and had already represented the town seven times in the legislature.[32]

Williams was of medium height and had well-proportioned features. "In his youth, his features were handsome, his hair and eyes were black, his nose aquiline, his face round, and his complexion fair." He was a persuasive and articulate writer and "a vehement and ardent orator." His voice was powerful, and passion increased his eloquence.

> His temper was naturally ardent, but his exertions to attain command over it were, in some degree, crowned with success. He possessed . . . a redundancy of spirit and vehemence of expression, which frequently created in himself, strong and sorrowful feelings. On ordinary occasions he was taciturn and reserved: he was involved habitually in deep thinking, and when he had formed his decision, was tenacious of his opinion.

His natural reserve was considered by some to be excessive pride. He is reputed to have never solicited a vote for himself and to have always voted according to the dictates of his conscience. In personal, business, and political life, his standards of conduct and integrity were extremely high. The high standards which he demanded of others, and his own deep piety, natural reserve, and taciturnity, however, gave him the reputation, particularly among those whose standards of behavior were lower, of being a self-rightous prig. This reputation was not entirely undeserved, for Williams had an absolute faith in the justice and virtue of his own position and was intolerant of those whose political opinions and motives seemed less pure than his own. He became a skillful political operator, particularly in forming backstage coalitions to further legislation he favored, legislation that accorded to the convictions of conscience and his own conception of the public welfare. A man of deep and abiding piety, he became Deacon of the First Church in 1768. He held rigidly to Congregational religious beliefs, was a strict and devoted churchgoer, and generously supported religious, educational, and charitable societies. He was interested in mechanical pursuits and architecture, but neither of these could be considered for a career. He also enjoyed the study of mathematics, and throughout his life he retained a proficiency in Greek and Latin. Despite, however, his broad interests and a political career that lasted fifty years, his political outlook always remained parochial. He never transcended the rural atmosphere of his youth, and he never travelled widely. Between graduation from Harvard and a trip to Philadelphia on behalf of the Council of Safety in September, 1775, only once did he leave Connecticut. He journeyed to Crown Point in the summer of 1761 on behalf of Trumbull and Company, a Lebanon-based group involved in military supply. He had few correspondents outside of Connecticut, and he never trusted people who were not New Englanders.[33]

Williams remained a bachelor until he was almost forty, but on February 14, 1771, he married Mary, second daughter of Governor Jonathan and Faith Robinson Trumbull. Williams had, however, an interest in marriage long before 1771. In March, 1761, he wrote a long romantic epistle to an unknown woman, a letter which he never sent. He expressed the conviction that "the happy Swain to whom thy Love is given, will pass thro Eden in his Road to Heaven," but he considered himself unworthy, primarily because of his lack of means. Writing to Joseph Trumbull, who had embarked on a business trip to England, he stated, "I believe Ladys are plenty in England, can't you pick out an agreable Wife? Were I in your Situation & had money enow to court with, wod try to find one." Williams had first highly regarded Jonathan Trumbull's elder daughter Faith, who married Jedidiah Huntington of Norwich on May 1, 1766. In January, 1765, in a letter which also may have been unsent, he revealed his esteem for a young lady who was bound to another. He congratulated her and went to to say:

> Were it otherwise I know a Gentlemen the strength, sincerity & ardor of whose first, last, only & undivided Affection for You . . . might perhaps excuse to himself the Hope of deserving Your Favor, but as his fortune is unequal to your Merits & just Expectations, suppose He will never give You any Trouble, but only to express (as by me he does) his most Cordial & ardent Wishes that You may attain ye completion of every kind of Felicity.

Solomon Williams was extremely pleased by his son's marriage. "All Events," he said, "are in the hands of God to whom I have Committed him . . . . Tis a bleasure [sic] to see a Prospect that mine After Me may have a Comfortable life."[34]

William Williams proved a conscientious, concerned, and loving husband and father. He regretted having to spend so much time away from his family, constantly worried about their health, and continually he chastised his wife for her failure to write. In the correspondence between husband and wife, a new portrait of Williams emerges. Instead of the dour but ardent and single-minded patriot, the human side of Williams is revealed. He is seen as a man who missed his wife, worried about the health and safety of his three children, was irked because he had run out of tobacco, was concerned about the care of his farm in his absence, and was worried about the health of his dearest Polly. He chastised his "dearest Love" constantly for her failure to write, and one time he noted with exasperation, when he heard that French officers were going to be quartered in his home, "I dont know what to make of it. I wish you had wrote me something about it & of any thing else. This is ye 4th or 5th Time I have wrote you without hearing a Word." Mary always rejoiced at hearing from her husband, but she found letter writing a great chore and thus did not write often herself. "I thank you for your long letter. I love to hear from you allways. . . . You can write three to my one & more good matter in half one of yours than a thousand of mine." She concluded with the tart comment, "dont say I never wrote you." The couple missed each other intensely. In September, 1776, while attending Congress, a duty Williams only reluctantly endured, he told of his great desire to return home. "My dear Love, I wish & long to see You, & if my Life is spared, I intend it before ye cold Season comes on, whether Mr. [Oliver] Wolcott relieves me or not." Mary expressed her love and longing in this way: "O what a Blessing I in joy in Such a husband & Father. . . . I never wish more for you than now." Although she survived her husband twenty years, Mary's health was uncertain, and William repeatedly told her to guard her health and not to overexert herself. On one occasion he advised Mary to take care of her teeth lest she lose them. In 1784, he told her that he had been urged to go to Congress, but had refused on her account. Another time he admonished her because she had almost become ill after attending "meeting" on foot. "I begd You not to do so."

> I beg & conjure You to use all possible Care & Prudence to avoid every Accident, Cold, or hardship, & to use all proper necessary Medicine. Your life & Health is You well know exceeding precious to me. . . . My Life without You wod be Bitterness & Anguish.[35]

The couple had three children, Solomon, born on January 5, 1772; Faith, born September 15, 1774; and William Trumbull, born September 7, 1779. Like most fathers, Williams constantly gave advice about them to his wife. He told their mother to let Faithy visit grandmother Williams and to be sure to "watch ye Children, Billy especially is always in Danger." Faith was named after grandmother Faith Trumbull and aunt Faith Huntington. In 1796, she married John McClellan, Yale

1785, a prominent Woodstock lawyer. William Trumbull was graduated from Yale in 1795, studied law, and settled permanently in his home town. Like his father, he represented Lebanon in the General Assembly. He married first cousin Sarah Trumbull, eldest child of David and Sarah Backus Trumbull, and died in Lebanon on December 16, 1839. Solly, however, was William Williams' favorite. Named after his father, Solomon was a precocious child, who suffered from poor health. At the age of ten, he passed Yale's entrance examination, although he did not enter until he reached sixteen. As a child, Solly was often sick. The boy was eleven when his father wrote, worriedly, "am concerned about Solly. You say the Medicines do no good. Am very sorry, but he is in ye hands of God & We must submit & hope & pray for mercy for him." When Solly was at college, his father searched all over Hartford for some garnet colored "Casamire for his Coat." The material was, he feared, "too gay," will "tend to make him proud," and "tend in some degree to divert his thoughts from ministerial Views." These anxieties proved unfounded, for young Solomon lived up to his father's hopes and expectations. A serious, virtuous youth, he returned to Lebanon and served four terms in the legislature between 1799 and 1803, but he preferred the ministry and began to study for it. Delicate health, however, forced him to give up these hopes, and in 1807 he removed to New York City. He decided that he could best serve the Christian faith through circulation of good literature, so he opened the Classical and Theological Bookstore, a favorite of the evangelical public. He died in New York on October 5, 1810, from typhus fever, an event that hastened the death of his bereaved father.[36]

New Light Politics and The Stamp Act Crisis

WILLIAM WILLIAMS entered politics in the midst of a struggle between New Lights and Old Lights for political control of the colony. Factionalism had existed prior to the Great Awakening, primarily in sectional disputes between east and west over economic development, but it had operated below the surface. The revival split the colony religiously and politically. Those most enthusiastic about the Great Revival, called New Lights, congregated in eastern Connecticut, but the ecclesiastical and political establishments were controlled by conservatives, who were repelled both by the emotional fervor of the New Lights and by their rejection of the principles of the Half-Way Covenant and the Saybrook Platform. Connecticut magistrates firmly allied themselves with opponents of the Awakening by a 1742 act against itineracy and a 1743 act repealing the 1708 Act of Toleration. These actions irretrievably entangled religion with politics. New Lights often disregarded the law, and both Solomon and Elisha Williams printed discourses condemning the law against itineracy. After attempting legally to silence their opponents, the Old Lights embarked on a political purge of the most outspoken supporters of the revival. Elisha Williams lost his seat on the Superior Court in 1743 and was dropped as Justice of the Peace one year later. Yet these efforts by Old Lights to crush their opponents failed, for persecution was sufficient to harass but not destroy, and too many powerful individuals aligned with the New Lights. Throughout the 1740s, New Lights endeavored to remove disabilities against them, and by the end of the decade they were gaining. In October, 1748, the Assembly appointed a committee to revise the colony's statutes. The Lower House nominated Elisha Williams, but the Upper House refused to concur. When the new law book appeared in 1750, the law against itineracy had disappeared.[1]

By 1750, the influence of the New Lights was increasing, and they began to attract the politically ambitious to their cause. Thomas Clap, the authoritarian Rector of Yale College, had been an inveterate enemy of revivalism in the 1740s, but he was soon won over to the New Lights by their increasing political power, and because, by the early 1750s, the New Lights appeared more religiously orthodox than Old Lights. A sign of Clap's change of allegiance came in 1749, when Solomon Williams, an eminent New Light and outspoken supporter of toleration for awakened ideas, was chosen a fellow of Yale College. Four years later, Clap offered Williams the post of Professor of Divinity. Williams reluctantly declined because he was too old, the endowment was insufficient, and because he was too religiously partisan to obtain the support of the legislature. By the end of the decade, New Lights usually commanded a majority in the Lower House and had commensurate support among the populace, but Governor Thomas Fitch and a majority of the twelve-man Council were Old Lights. Some day, whether through attrition or a political coup, it was evident that the New Lights would capture this last Old Light bastion, because secular discontent and religious piety continued to strengthen the New Light cause. Their support centered in New London and Windham Counties, and by 1760 they represented a powerful but heterogenous political and religious coalition. Paper money advocates, new and less-established merchants, and the chief supporters of the Susquehannah Company were strongest in eastern Connecticut. Here, too, the Great Awakening had made its greatest impact. Religiously, the New Lights consisted of three branches. The New Divinity branch comprised the spiritual heirs of Jonathan Edwards, and was noted for its piety and devotion to Calvinist doctrine. The Orthodoxy branch, led by Rector Clap, aimed at stamping out heresy at Yale and in New Haven County. The largest and most influential branch was the "eastern" one—pious, fervent, favoring religious toleration, and combining economic interest with religious zeal.[2]

Born and raised in eastern Connecticut and the son of an eminent New Light, William Williams naturally identified with the New Lights. In 1759, he became involved in an abortive attempt to remove Governor Fitch and seven Old Light Councillors from office. A religious dispute in Wallingford gave the insurgents an issue which they hoped to exploit for their political advantage. Daniel Lyman, a prominent New Haven New Light, wrote Williams about the plan. He esteemed Williams for his concern for "the Calvinistical Intrest & the Religious Constitution of this Govt.," and believed that Williams would do everything in his "Power to help forward the Importent Design." Lyman hoped that like-minded individuals in both the eastern and western sections of the colony would unite "to put our Publick Affairs both Civil & Sacred on a more Solid & Safe Foundation, and not forever be obliged to Truckle to a few Designing Men on the other side of the Question." The plan fell through, but other New Light efforts were crowned with success in 1759 and 1760. Their campaign to secure toleration and recognition for Separate churches in Canterbury, Plainfield, and White Haven succeeded, while the Assembly also acquiesced to demands by Wallingford New Lights to be incorporated into a distinct ecclesiastical society. Not until the passage of the Stamp Act, however, would New Lights be given the opportunity to expel their opponents from the citadels of power.[3]

*

The Assembly first appointed William Williams a Justice of the Peace for Windham County in May, 1759, along with cousins Ebenezer and Thomas Williams of Pomfret and Ebenezer West, William Metcalf, Joseph Fowler, and Joseph Clark of Lebanon. Another measure of his increasing reputation occurred in October, when the Assembly appointed Jonathan Trumbull, Christopher Avery, and Williams a committee to investigate a petition of Solomon Drown et al, who claimed that one David Nevins, deceased, had defrauded them through execution of a false bill of sale to prevent seizure of his land by creditors. The committee reported in May, 1760, and agreed that the sale was fraudulent. The Assembly ordered that redress be given the memorialists.[4]

In March, 1761, when the French and Indian War was drawing to a close, the Assembly granted Jonathan Trumbull and Hezekiah Huntington, a Councillor from Norwich, a contract to supply Connecticut troops with clothing and refreshments. Trumbull and Huntington soon realized that the task of supplying twenty-three hundred men was too great to execute alone, and so, on June 5, 1761, they entered into a covenant with Colonel Eleazar Fitch of Windham, John Ledyard of Hartford, and William Williams. The partnership was called Trumbull and Company, and each partner was to receive two-ninths of the profits, except Williams, who had a one-ninth share.[5] This endeavor was the largest business activity that Williams was to engage in during his years as a merchant.

The first teams carrying provisions arrived in Albany on June 17, but from the very beginning, Trumbull and Company encountered difficulties. Teams proved difficult to secure, and the selection of goods was poor. The partners sent too much rum and too little foodstuffs. Personal animosities compounded existing difficulties. Captain Nathaniel Porter of Lebanon attempted to discredit the company, and he did succeed in arousing a great deal of dissatisfaction. Porter had a grudge against Trumbull and Company, an animosity directed primarily at Jonathan Trumbull. Porter, born and raised in Lebanon, had been graduated from Yale in 1749. He became a physician, and he served in that capacity in the 1755 campaign against the French. In 1756, Porter was appointed Captain of the Fourth Company of the regiment commanded by David Wooster. The Lower House nominated Porter to command a company in the 1758 campaign, but the Upper House, in which both Trumbull and Huntington served, refused to concur. Joshua Barker of Lebanon was appointed in his stead. During the 1759 campaign, Porter served as a sutler for Connecticut troops, a position which he sought again in 1761. He petitioned the Assembly and asserted that he had provided provisions in past campaigns and had expected to continue, but had been prevented from doing so by the contract with Trumbull and Huntington. Although he offered to supply food thirty per cent cheaper and clothing forty-five per cent cheaper than Trumbull and Company, the petition was turned down. Porter's career had been frustrated in two instances by the Assembly, disappointments that Porter could attribute to personal acquaintances. Mentally unstable and believing himself wrongfully persecuted, Porter journeyed north to exact revenge on the persons he held responsible for his ill-fortune.[6]

William Williams arrived in Albany in the last week of June, and he endeavored to aid Colonel Fitch in neutralizing Porter's charges. Porter, like one who was "Crazy" and seeking "to serve his Revenge," was rendered harmless, although he continued plotting against Trumbull and Company. Williams remained in the Hudson

Valley for another month and a half, attempting to further the Company's cause. The Company became involved in further difficulties because of the excessively large quantities of alcoholic beverages the contractors had brought. General Amherst was "in a terrible Passion yt so much Rum is got along to ye Connect[icut] troops & posstively refus'd a Pass to ye Province Sutlers for any Spirits." Amherst ordered that no more rum be provided Connecticut troops, and Colonel Haviland, commandant at Crown Point, seized all alcoholic beverages at the post. Williams considered Haviland, a man "every One seems to hate," responsible for the infamous order.[7]

Williams returned to Lebanon in mid-August. His contacts with the British army had not been congenial. As John Sanderson once declared:

> He [William Williams] returned dissatisfied and disgusted with the British commanders: their haughtiness, and arbitrary conduct, and their inattention to the interests of America, made a powerful and lasting impression on his mind. Even at that early period, he formed the opinion that the prosperity of his native country would never be secured under the administration of officers who had no common interests nor feelings with the people; and that, to enable them to profit by the means within their reach, a government dependent on themselves, was necessary.

Sanderson exaggerated the effect of this experience on Williams' mind, since his New Light sentiments most strongly determined his political posture. Williams disliked Colonel Haviland and the British attitude of condescension towards colonials. Some officers acted mad either for the sake of it, from a spirit of envy, or because "the Devil is in some of e'm." He particularly deplored the British attitude towards contractors. "Contractors do not look upon Themselves . . . to be kick'd abt by petty Officers."[8] Although Williams' contact with Britain was not pleasant, still it did no more than reinforce his parochialism and his trust in America's virtue, a belief that was the product of his entire life and experience.

*

The French and Indian War ended in 1763. Great Britain emerged victorious, but burdened with a national debt of £130,000,-000. As part of imperial reorganization, the British ministry resolved to tighten the acts of trade to effect, once and for all, the commercial subordination of the colonies to the assumptions of mercantilism. In keeping with this new direction in imperial policy, the Grenville ministry planned, notwithstanding the removal of the French menace, to station a permanent, ten thousand-man army in the colonies. The government believed the colonies should pay part of the expenses.

Connecticut's opposition to the new course of British policy was decisive and violent, but it is easier to show what happened after 1763 than explain why. Oscar Zeichner, author of the best work on eighteenth-century Connecticut politics, focused on the sectional split between east and west and the colony's economic difficulties after the French and Indian War. The Great Awakening and the activities of the Susquehannah Company, as Zeichner saw it, destroyed the colony's political homogeneity. The chief proponents of both concentrated in Windham and New London Counties. A severe depression struck Connecticut after the defeat of the French, and, by 1765, colony taxpayers were £80,000 in arrears of colony taxes. The British government chose this inopportune moment to levy stamp duties on the American colonies. Connecticut freeholders would have been seriously affected by these new impositions, even if the colony had been enjoying prosperity, but, in the midst of economic depression, the people were in no mood to pay additional taxes. Both conservative Old Lights and eastern New Lights opposed the Stamp Act, but, after its passage, conservatives like Governor Thomas Fitch and Jared Ingersoll bowed to the inevitable. They believed in the supremacy of Parliament and felt that the colonists were obligated to submit. New Light-dominated eastern Connecticut, however, continued to resist. New Lights and Old Lights "had been grinding their axes for some time," and the election of 1766, which saw the defeat of Governor Fitch, gave the New Lights "the opportunity to cut off the political heads of some of their old opponents."[9]

Richard L. Bushman, author of *From Puritan to Yankee,* added a new dimension toward understanding the problem. He correctly emphasized the split between New Lights and Old Lights. New Light agitation was in part due to previous grudges, and the insensitivity of Old Lights to popular rage provided an opportunity to oust long-detested opponents. But to attribute New Light agitation solely to long-standing feuds was to misjudge their fervor and intensity. Both factions detested the Stamp Act, but their differing responses, when faced with accomplished fact, lay in their contrasting world views. The Old Light world revolved around traditional concepts of social order. "Its members derived personal security from the belief that authority, descending from above through the agencies of government, could keep the peace." Although willing to tolerate limited conflicts, a threat to overturn the entire political fabric forced them to become advocates of order and to submit to the authority of Parliament. New Lights did not hold government in such awe. They had opposed the rulers of government since the Great Awakening, and defiance of the colonial government had become almost habitual. Hence, for New Lights, the transition from resistance to Connecticut magistrates to resistence to the crown marked an almost natural progression.[10]

Further insight into the New Light mentality can be derived from Bernard Bailyn's striking interpretation of the intellectual origins of the American Revolution. Bailyn argues that the dominant strain of political thought in the colonies was derived from radical political and social thought of the English Civil War and from a small group of eighteenth-century radical publicists who were the transmitters of this tradition. The adherents of this dissenting view of politics stressed the incompatibility of liberty and power. Power was aggressive and ever expanding; liberty was passive. Threats to liberty lurked in the designs of magistrates in office to aggrandize their power by corruption and thereby destroy the balance of the English constitution. In Britain, this opposition view of politics was embraced by only a small minority, but the altered conditions of life and politics in the New World made what were only theoretical dangers to liberty in Britain appear to be real dangers in the colonies. In Connecticut, the New Lights had struggled for twenty years to overcome the political dominance of the Old Lights. New Lights were dissenters *par excellence*, and they, far more than their opponents, viewed British policy after 1763 not merely as mistaken, but as a deliberate conspiracy aiming at the destruction of liberty as well. As dissenters accustomed to resisting authority, the New Lights saw much more clearly the direction of British policy and the dangers this represented to American liberties and Connecticut's charter, and thus they were much more willing to resist Parliament than their conservative adversaries.[11]

Even before the Sugar Act became law in 1764, Connecticut traders united to oppose it. On January 20, 1764, New London merchants asked the Assembly to protest the proposed act. At a special session of the legislature in March, a committee headed by Jonathan Trumbull was appointed "to take into consideration what they should think expedient for the Assembly to do, in order to prevent the revival of the act of Parliament laying a duty on foreign sugar and molasses." The committee urged Richard Jackson, Connecticut's agent in London, to use his influence to prevent passage of the bill. Three prominent New London merchants were commissioned to draw up arguments against the measure, and another committee that included William Williams was appointed in May. These protests, however, availed nothing. The Sugar Act took the form of a revision of the acts of trade, but the purpose was new. Heretofore, Parliament had levied duties for the purpose of regulating trade, but the new levies were aimed at raising a revenue to help defray the cost of maintaining British troops in North America.[12].

Meeting in October, the Assembly protested an even more threatening proposal by the Grenville ministry, a plan to levy stamp duties on the American colonies. The previous May, the Assembly had chosen a committee consisting of Ebenezer Silliman, Jared Ingersoll, and George Wyllys, all stout conservatives, to assist the Governor in collecting "all such arguments and objections as may justly and reasonably be advanced against creating and collecting a Revenue in America . . . and especially against effecting the same by Stamp Duties." The result of these deliberations was a document entitled "Reasons why the British Colonies in America should not be charged with Internal Taxes by Authority of Parliament." The tone of the protest was moderate, yet the report, approved by the Assembly, gave no doubt that the colony was determined to defend its charter rights and liberties. British subjects could be rightfully taxed only by the legally-elected representatives of the people. A stamp tax, or any other internal tax, violated Connecticut's charter rights. But the colony confined its objections to internal taxes and failed to consider whether Parliament could use trade regulations as a source of revenue, the problem raised by the Sugar Act. At the same time, the Assembly resolved to appoint Jared Ingersoll to assist the regular colony agent in opposing the Stamp Act. Connecticut's cautious response to the proposed stamp tax showed that the colony was still controlled by conservative elements.[13]

The Stamp Act became law in March, 1765, and almost everything written or printed, from diplomas and deeds to newspapers and playing cards, required stamps. Since Parliament kindly delayed the date of execution for the Act until November 1, 1765, Americans had six months to prepare resistance. In Connecticut, the Stamp Act widened the deep split between Old Lights and New Lights. Conservatives like Governor Fitch and Ingersoll, who became Stamp Distributor for Connecticut, believed that Parliament was supreme and, whatever their personal sentiments, that the law had to be obeyed. New Lights, however, continued to resist. The Sons of Liberty, whose leaders belonged to the "Eastern Faction," spearheaded the opposition.[14] Israel Putnam of Pomfret, Hugh Ledlie of Windham, and John Durkee of Norwich stood at the forefront of the Sons. Other eastern men of standing connected with the organization were Matthew Griswold and the Reverend Stephen Johnson of Lyme, Jabez and Jedidiah Huntington of Norwich, Eliphalet Dyer of Windham, Jonathan Trumbull, and William Williams.[15]

On August 14, Massachusetts Stamp Distributor Andrew Oliver was hanged in effigy and his property vandalized. He resigned the following day. Connecticut patriots soon followed Boston's example. Ingersoll was hanged in effigy in Norwich on August 21, in New London the next day, in Windham and Lebanon on August 26, and in Lyme on the twenty-ninth.[16] In Lebanon, all public buildings were draped in black, and a special trial was held for the criminal, the "late A—t for this Colony," who appeared "in the Person of his VIRTUAL Representative." He was denied none of his rights as an Englishman, and, upon conviction, was sentenced to be "hanged by the Neck 'til dead" and "afterwards to be committed to the Flames, that if possible he might be purified by Fire." The sentence was executed before a huge crowd "of Spectators exulting in the Prospect of Liberty." Accompanying the prisoner to the execution site were the "grand Seducer of Mankind," who proposed that he accept his "Office and Inslave your Country and 40£ per Annum shall be your Reward," and a lady in chains representing his injured country. The lady pleaded with "her base, unnatural Child" to remember his country, but the degenerate replied, "Perish my Country, so that I get that Reward."[17]

Trumbull urged Governor Fitch to call a special session of the legislature so that it could elect delegates to the Stamp Act Congress. Trumbull stated emphatically that the "People in this part of the Colony are very Jealous for their Liberties and Desire That The Most Vigorous Exertions be made for the Repeal of the Late Act of Parliament." Freeman's meetings in Lebanon and neighboring towns had "Unanimously shewn their Minds . . . In This Critical & Dangerous Situation," for they considered the Stamp Act "utterly subversive to their Rights & Privileges."[18] The Sons of Liberty had two goals at this juncture. They wanted a special session of the legislature to send delegates to the Stamp Act Congress, and they were determined to force Jared Ingersoll to resign. Both objectives were achieved within a month. On September 19, 1765, some five hundred Sons of Liberty from New London and Windham Counties, led by John Durkee, intercepted Ingersoll at Wethersfield and forced him to resign. The special session of the legislature convened the same day, and the delegates were obviously impressed by the incident, for the Assembly resolved to send Eliphalet Dyer, William Samuel Johnson, and David Rowland to the Congress. Conservative elements still had enough control over the situation, however, to instruct the delegates not to sign any document that would bind the colony.[19]

Although his presence is not always apparent, Williams lived at the center of those political activities in 1765 and 1766 that culminated in the defeat of Governor Fitch and his Old Light allies. He sardonically asserted that Americans had always been intended "by our dear Mothr Country to be Her Slaves." In the seventeenth century, because they had been "judged unworthy to enjoy the Liberty of Conscience in matters of Religion," they had left England and tamed the wilderness. Through unremitting toil, they had prospered, and "their kind Mother blessed them" with Navigation Acts to ensure that England could secure the profits of their labor. Now that the French had been pushed out of Canada, Britain had decided that Americans should be taxed to help discharge the national debt. Britain's action was just only "because We ran away from her Oppressions at home & have impudently taken upon us to enjoy the Privileges of Englishmen, altho we had then Royal License to do so." Jared Ingersoll, too, had behaved correctly. It would have been foolish for him to have "stood out & insisted on his Country's being Freemen, tho they were not born Slaves." It was only proper for Americans to share in the spoils. The stampmaster, he concluded, "has acted a prudent part, & can't imagine He deserves to be virtually hang'd & burn't in so many Places. It might surely be Punishment enough if [he] were really hang'd in any One."[20]

The Assembly met in regular session on October 10, 1765, and was dominated by opponents of the Stamp Act. The deputies were "deeply concerned at [the] tremendous Evils connected" with the Stamp Act, and they "firmly resolved if possible to avoid them."[21] The legislature quickly approved the resolves adopted by the Stamp Act Congress and proceeded to adopt its own resolutions. The Act violated Connecticut's charter and deprived residents of the colony of the fundamental rights of Englishmen. The lawmakers affirmed that their birth in the New World did not deprive them of the liberties and immunities of native-born Englishmen. "That, in the opinion of this House, an act for raising money by duties or taxes . . . is always considered as a free gift of the people made by their legal and elected representatives." The only legal representatives of the inhabitants of Connecticut were the people they elected to the General Assembly; therefore, the Stamp Act was "unprecedented and unconstitutional." These resolves, drafted by William Williams, were approved in the Lower House by a vote of eighty-five to five. A majority in the Council also approved.[22]

Williams, a veteran legislator and a leading radical, reported on the doings of the Assembly to his friend Daniel Lyman of New Haven. The House, after considerable debate, passed their resolves concerning the Stamp Act with an "Entry signifying ye unanimity of ye H[ouse] & desire yt yy might be enter'd on ye Records & remain on ye Files of ye G. Assembly, for which ye Concure[nce] of ye U[pper] H[ouse] was necessary." Governor Fitch, however, used his influence to ensure that the resolves were not acted upon by the Council until the last day of the session. At this juncture, the Lower House prevailed upon the Upper House to act, and that body finally "concurd w[it]h what we desired ye Great Chair & 4 Elbows excepted."[23] The Assembly also gave its approval to an address to the King, Commons, and Lords drawn up by the Stamp Act Congress and sent special instructions to Richard Jackson, in which they ordered him "by no means to acknowledge ye Right of Parl[iament] to impose inter[nal] Taxes."[24]

The Stamp Act required all magistrates to take an oath to uphold its provisions. Governor Fitch, conservative by instinct and repelled by violence and disunity, at the last moment, along with Old Light Councillors, Ebenezer Silliman, John Chester, Jabez Hamlin, and Benjamin Hall, took the required oath. This act, the most critical in Connecticut's political history, meant political suicide for the oathtakers and the final triumph for the New Light party. The atmosphere in New Haven was supercharged with emotion as the November 1 deadline approached. "Various & sundry Disputes in ye Council" took place over the Stamp Act oath. Fitch "from ye first descovered his firm resolution to take . . . it," and he utterly refused to take contrary advice from the Lower House. He informed the Council that "he did not want their nor any Bodys advice, as ye asking it wod imply a doubt in his mind, but he had none." The Council majority refused to take the oath and vainly tried to persuade the Governor and the four recalcitrants to administer the oath outside the Council chamber, because they "cod not willingly be present." The Governor insisted that the action be performed in the chamber, so the majority withdrew, leaving the Governor, his four allies, and Elisha Sheldon, who could not make up his mind, behind in the room. The House was immediately informed, and the uproar reminded Williams of Milton's description of Eve plucking the fruit from the forbidden tree. The colony was thrown "into great Consternation & Agony." The commotions were particularly acute on the "Eastern Shores." Williams stated that among the most rash and zealous there was a good deal of talk "of waiting on ye Govr. & his 4 Friends in a very respectable Body (as to Nos) & They undoubtedly were . . . greatly terrified at ye Reports." The Sons of Liberty were determined, however, "to turn them all out of yr places." The Governor and his allies, wrote William Williams, "may certainly expect political death."[25]

After November 1, the Sons of Liberty pursued three goals. They wanted to ensure that no stamps were distributed anywhere in Connecticut, they wished to maintain popular wrath against "Stamping Oppression," and they aimed at purging their political opponents. They achived each of these aims. Popular hostility to the stamp tax continued to increase, and, in the months that followed, popular meetings run by the Sons superseded regular governments, particularly in eastern Connecticut. On November 11, 1765, representatives from eastern towns met in Windham and resolved to oppose distribution of stamps and to maintain "union, harmony and good agreement" in opposing the Stamp Act. They also recommended that each county call a meeting every month until the Act was repealed. A New London County meeting was to be convened on November 19 and the convention for the whole of Windham County on November 26.[26]

Jared Ingersoll's troubles had not yet ended, for hostility towards him was intense. His activities were monitored closely in order that any further treasonable activity could be used to increase popular hatred of both the Stamp Act and the Connecticut conservatives. The Sons soon learned that Ingersoll was carrying on a correspondence with English friends. Colonel Israel Putnam, acting as head of the Sons of Liberty, called a meeting in Windham in late November, and between three and four thousand persons attended. They decided to send a committee to meet with the stamp master for the purpose of demanding an explanation for his conduct. Captains Hugh Ledlie, Aaron Cleaveland of Canterbury, and Azel Fitch of Lebanon travelled to New Haven "to examine some private Letters . . . of our Stamp man to his Friends, Jackson & Whately & ye Comis: of Stamps."[27] Ingersoll denied acting unpatriotically, and the three delegates declared themselves satisfied. But they asked permission to take his correspondence back to Windham, and Ingersoll, fearing the "innuendos, if he shod refuse," consented. Another special meeting convened in Windham on December 12, and Eliphalet Dyer read the letters to the vast multitude. Ingersoll gave a summary of proceedings relative to the Stamp Act and "told most things freely, but all too much in ye Language of anger, Chargrin & Resentment." Unfortunately for Ingersoll, some of his statements were twisted and then printed in the *New London Gazette*, an action that further inflamed passions against him, so that he was finally compelled to promise to write nothing more to Britain without permission of the Sons.[28]

Additional meetings were held throughout eastern Connecticut in the winter of 1765-1766. On December 24, there was one in Pomfret in order to further "animate & strengthen in ye People an Aversion & abhorrence of Stamping Oppression." On January 13, 1766, Sons of Liberty from eastern Connecticut gathered in Lyme. The delegates demanded that normal commercial and legal business be renewed without using stamps, and they also discussed a possible slate of candidates to oppose the Old Light incumbents. The climax of the activities of the Sons of Liberty came at a colonywide meeting in Hartford on March 25 and 26, at which the two eastern counties were much more fully-represented than were the other parts of the colony. Lebanon, however, did not send delegates. But this did not mean that the Lebanon townspeople were motivated by any "want of a fix'd & unalterable attachment to yt important, glorious & common cause of Liberty, which has so nobly animated the Breasts of every one deserving ye name of an Englishman." William Williams, writing on behalf of Lebanon's Sons of Liberty, informed the delegates that they did not send representatives because they had accidentally failed to give proper notice for a meeting to select them. Few persons attended the meeting, so they decided not to choose delegates, but rather to express their sentiments by pen. Williams affirmed that submission to Britain "must involve a greater Evil than can be the Consequence of a persevering & unshaken Resolution . . . to be free." He applauded the "noble spirited & generous Love of heaven born Liberty, which every order of Men . . . have descover'd Themselves to be inspird withall." He likewise condemmed the "Conduct of those Few . . . who thro Fear or from worse Motives, wo'd not have made one feeble Attempt to preserve that Freedom, in defense of whose Cause, Rivers of human Blood have been deservedly shed." Had the conduct of these traitors been generally imitiated, slavery would by now have "spread its baneful & desolating Influence over the fruitful Fields of America." Williams asked for a copy of the proceedings, and he concluded with the belief that the local Sons would heartily concur in the results.[29]

The Sons of Liberty Convention, attended by delegates "from a great Majority of the Towns," approved several perfunctory resolutions affirming their loyalty to the king, and giving their "respectful approbation" of the resolves passed by the General Assembly the past October. The delegates then appointed a nine-man committee to correspond with Sons in other colonies. Next, they moved on to the true purpose of the gathering: to consider "wheter a Change in the Ministry . . . might not be necessary among us." Meeting in closed session, the delegates firmed up their plans to replace their political opponents in the upcoming election. The convention was dominated by delegates from Windham and New London Counties, and their will prevailed. In order to ensure the defeat of the Old Lights, eastern radicals needed support from the west. In December, 1765, Eliphalet Dyer began corresponding with William Samuel Johnson of Stratford, proposing an alliance between eastern radicals and Fairfield County Anglicans.[30] Consummation of this bargain and, far more importantly, the overwhelming strength of the Sons of Liberty in eastern Connecticut, culminated in the decisive defeat of Governor Fitch and the four Old Light Councillors. Deputy-Governor William Pitkin became Governor, and Jonathan Trumbull, the senior Assistant, was elevated to Deputy-Governor. Six new Assistants were elected, among them William Pitkin, Jr., former Clerk of the House and Clerk of the Sons of Liberty Convention, Roger Sherman, and William Samuel Johnson, the first Anglican to sit on the Council.[31] As a reward for his exertions in the cause of liberty, William Williams, too, gathered political fruits. His peers in the Lower House elected him Clerk, the second most important position in that body, and he was chosen Major of the Twelfth Militia Regiment.[32] The Stamp Act had been repealed by the time the legislature convened, and a committee of twelve persons, including the new Deputy-Governor and William Williams, was appointed to assist the Governor in preparing an address to the king expressing the gratitude of the colony for the happy turn of events.[33]

✿

At the age of thirty-five, Williams had already achieved marked success in politics, and during the next decade his importance was to increase steadily in radical ranks. From the outset of the Revolutionary era, he was an unswerving believer in the rightousness of the American cause. A measure of his reputation can be seen in the number of important committees on which he served and in the commissions he executed on behalf of the General Assembly over the next few years. In October, 1766, the Assembly appointed Williams, Deputy-Governor Trumbull, Matthew Griswold, and George Wyllys to look into the Mohegan Case and prepare the colony's defense.[34] In May of 1767, Williams and five others were appointed Auditors of colonial accounts. The Assembly reappointed him Auditor on six other occasions.[35] The legislature designated Williams and two others in October to lay out "a shorter and more feasible road" between New Haven and Windham via Branford, Durham, Middletown, East Haddam, and Lebanon. He was also chosen, along with Hezekiah Huntington and Joseph Spencer, to investigate the sorrowful circumstances in the Second Society in Lyme, which for six years had been "destitute of a regular gospel ministry," and to consider a petition of Lyme Baptists, who wished to be formed into a distinct ecclesiastical society.[36] In January, 1769, after the resignation of Treasurer Joseph Talcott, John Ledyard, former partner in Trumbull and Company, and William Williams were selected to receive from Talcott the money in his hands belonging to the colony and all other accounts in his possession and deliver them to John Lawrence, the new Treasurer. The legislature also appointed Williams to a committee to investigate a New London lottery. In October, 1769, he served on a committee to see to the collection of arrears in colonial taxes collected by William Starr of Middletown, deceased. The Assembly granted Williams £22 in October, 1770, to secure passage to England for one Thomas Simonds, a transient, and a Mr. and Mrs. Griffith Meredith of Lebanon, persons incapable of supporting themselves and wishing to return home. The Assembly chose Williams and Joseph Trumbull in May, 1771, to collect evidence for determining the boundary line between Massachusetts and Connecticut, and between May, 1771, and October, 1773, he served on five other committees to which he was appointed by the General Assembly.[37]

Representatives, particularly those with seniority, were often chosen to act for the colony by serving on committees. These duties may have been tedious and time consuming, but such service was necessary for the proper functioning of government, and, moreover, they provided a means for young and ambitious politicians to prove their merits. Committee work gave Williams an opportunity to earn his stripes and prepare the way for higher public service. Since these committees travelled throughout the colony to carry out their mandates, the young legislator was also given the opportunity of gaining a wider reputation. Williams' service on behalf of the New Lights and the Sons of Liberty between 1759 and 1766 culminated in his election as Clerk of the House and appointment as Major of the Twelfth Regiment. Continued legislative service after 1765 and continued leadership in Patriot ranks prepared Williams for more crucial responsibilities as the Revolutionary crisis drew nearer.

The Coming of the Revolution

Connecticut's joy over the repeal of the Stamp Act was short-lived. Chancellor of the Exchequer Charles Townshend, in the spring of 1767, persuaded Parliament to levy new taxes on the American colonies in the hopes of gaining money from them painlessly. Parliament mistakenly believed that Americans had objected to internal taxation, but not to external taxation or to duties imposed on trade. Americans *had*, in fact, distinguished between taxation and legislation. Legislation was a function of sovereignty, and Parliament could legally regulate the commerce and trade of the empire. But "an act for raising money by duties or taxes differs from other acts of legislation in that it is always considered as a free gift of the people made by their legal and elected representatives." Seizing on a distinction which he thought absurd, Townshend decided to saddle America with external taxes on goods imported into the colonies. These duties were levied on glass, lead, paints, paper, and, most significantly, tea, and, to ensure that the requisite duties would be collected and the colonial habit of smuggling would be repressed, Townshend reorganized the customs service.[1]

Boston again took the lead in mobilizing resistance. The inhabitants resolved on October 28, 1767, to make new efforts to promote home manufactures and non-consumption of British goods, and they sent copies of their resolutions to towns in Massachusetts and the neighboring colonies. Town meetings in Windham, Ashford, Canterbury, and Plainfield quickly endorsed Boston's position. The inhabitants of Lebanon, meeting on December 7, also endorsed the measures taken at Boston "to promote & encourage ye Manufactures" and to cease purchasing "superfluous & costly Articles imported here to fore." Deputy-Governor Trumbull, William Williams, Vetch Williams, and six others were appointed to act by themselves and in concert with committees in neighboring towns "to consider of & devise such Measures & Means as may most effectually tend to promote & encourage Industry, Economy, & Manufactures."[2]

Pennsylvania's John Dickinson, author of "Letters from a Farmer," penned the most persuasive objections to the Townshend duties. Parliament had the legal right, wrote Dickinson, to levy duties to regulate trade, but not to use duties for the purpose of raising revenue. The freemen of Lebanon on April 11, 1768, fervently endorsed the "Farmer's" statements and addressed a letter written to him by Town Clerk Williams. The freemen felt greatly distressed by Parliament's recent acts whereby, for the expressed purpose of raising a revenue for the crown, their property was taken without their consent. They were, therefore, pleased by the efforts of "The Farmer" in the "glorious Cause of endanger'd Liberty." He had "vindicated the rights of America," had warned on the infinite danger of "indolent Acquiescence in Principles, which, extended to their genuine Length, will end in a total Subversion of her Constitutional Freedom," and his eloquence had strengthened the hands "of the generous Multitude engaged in that noble Cause." At the same meeting, the freemen issued instructions to their representatives, William Williams and Captain William Sims. The recent acts of Parliament granted away their property without their consent, were contrary to the British constitution, and sapped the foundations of American liberty. Lebanon's deputies were enjoined to exert themselves to urge the Assembly to petition the king, portraying the grievances Americans were enduring and to secure "relief from the unconstitutional burdens imposed upon us." The delegates were also instructed to discourage the importation of unnecessary articles of consumption and to encourage frugality, industry, and home manufactures.[3]

Eastern towns had again been the first to act in opposing these new threats to American liberty. The colonial government took no action until spring, when the Assembly gave indirect support to the non-importation movement by levying a five per cent duty on goods imported into the colony by non-resident merchants. On June 10, however, the last day of the session, a memorial was addressed to the king, together with letters to agent Richard Jackson, agent William Samuel Johnson, and Lord Hillsborough, Secretary of State for the American Department. The colony petitioned the king for relief from the Townshend duties, taxes which violated Connecticut's charter rights and the liberties of free and natural-born Englishmen. By the fall of 1769, Connecticut traders had subscribed to non-importation agreements adopted by merchants in Boston, New York, and Philadelphia.[4]

The Board of Customs Commissioners, created to enforce the laws of trade, and with headquarters in Boston, proved to be a major source of damage to Anglo-American relations between 1768 and 1772. During this "era of customs racketeering," a new breed of tactless, arbitrary, and mercenary customs officers, by their unequal and vindictive enforcement of the Navigation Acts, precipitated a riot in June, 1768, after seizing John Hancock's *Liberty*. Britain promptly responded by dispatching four regiments of regulars to Boston to uphold authority.[5] These events caused prescient observers like Solomon Williams and Jonathan Trumbull to observe that "Dark Clouds" were hanging over England and America.[6] William Williams sarcastically castigated Britain as "our Step Mother Country." The colonies were "much united & I dare prophesie [they] will be more & more so, in a firm, unshaken & unalterable Opinion that the British House of Commons have no right to tax them." The colonies would willingly remain dependent, if only Britain would recognize their rights and liberties, but, should she persist in her present policy, the future "will be dreadfully unhappy for Both." Connecticut would "stand fast forever" in defense of its liberties, and although Williams professed to believe that the British would not "draw the Sword on their own Children," if they should, "Our Blood is more at their Service than our Liberties."[7]

In response to the occupation of Boston, a very full meeting of the inhabitants of Lebanon convened on September 26. Distressed by the arrival of troops and the unhappy circumstances with regard to America's precious constitutional rights and privileges, the inhabitants unanimously expressed their "most hearty union in sentiments with our brethren in Boston." They vowed they would always remonstrate firmly against all acts imposing duties on them without their consent and resolved to exert themselves in every lawful, reasonable, and constitutional way to uphold their liberties and privileges.[8]

By the summer of 1769, even radicals like Williams were satisfied with the support in Connecticut for non-importation. Williams noted that Councillor Hezekiah Huntington was "a good deal shook" by a rumor that he had imported British goods. If the story had been true and generally known, Williams wrote, "it wo'd without doubt have proved fatal to his Station." Had not Williams still retained some affection for the mother country, he would be happy if the Townshend Acts were never repealed. Americans had loved English manufactured goods far too much, but now, happily, the situation had changed. The people "seem to have lost their fondness for Them" and vie to see "who shall run fastest into home manufactures." Lebanon's grammar school educated a number of children of the most prominent men in Georgia and the Carolinas, and their "Fathers have given orders that They be clad wholly in manufactures of this Country." The merchants, too, Williams joyfully concluded, also "seem honestly resolved to adhere to their resolutions of non-importation."[9]

The Lower House in October adopted a resolution approving of non-importation "until the revenue laws are repealled." In January, 1770, Williams again asserted that a strict adherence to non-importation was of vital importance to help save the country from "compleat Slavery." Unfortunately, however, a few merchants began "to stagger," and Williams feared that disaffection was spreading. If the merchants deserted the cause, only the people, "the last & only sure Recourse," could bring traders back to the paths of virtue. Lebanon, fortunately, contained no persons disposed to violate the non-importation agreements. The town was "almost to a Man fixed & united in ye constitutio[na]l Principles of Liberty & are ever ready to take any proper steps in Vindication of them."[10]

On March 5, 1770, an event known in history as the Boston Massacre occurred. A small detachment of soldiers guarding the customs-house was set upon by a mob. The frightened soldiers fired, and five rioters died.[11] The massacre, which confirmed all colonial fears about the evils of standing armies, caused the inhabitants of Lebanon, on April 9, speaking through William Williams, to again express their sentiments on the evils recurring around them. They repeated that they were tenaciously attached to their rights and liberties, and that they viewed with sincere grief the distresses the nation endured "in consequence of measures planned by a few artful, designing men." They particularly deplored the unhappy fate of Boston, subjected to the imposition of a standing army among them. The soldiers had been responsible for a "great variety of Evils and Distresses to that most loyal people, and lately . . . of the barbarous Murder of a number of the inhabitants of that Town." In the midst of these calamities, the inhabitants rejoiced in the harmony and union of the American people in defense of their liberties. They praised the patriotic conduct of the merchants and vowed to do their utmost to promote useful manufacture.[12]

A new government in Britain, headed by Lord North, decided on a strategic retreat in the face of protests by British merchants and colonial resistance. No one in authority thought highly of the Townshend duties and, except for the one on tea, they were all repealed. The government retained the duty on that commodity as a symbol of Parliamentary authority, and, since Americans loved tea, they could, perhaps, be seduced into purchasing it. The partial repeal of the Townshend duties destroyed the non-importation agreements. Merchants in New York City voted to resume importation of all goods except tea, and merchants in other major ports quickly followed suit. The farmers of eastern Connecticut, however, condemned this sacrifice of principle for profit. They held many meetings in a fruitless attempt to devise more effective means of enforcing the non-importation agreements. Merchants in Hartford, Middletown, and New Haven condemned the unpatriotic conduct of the New Yorkers, and a general convention was held in New Haven on September 13 in which all Windham County towns were represented.[13]

On August 27, 1770, the townspeople in Lebanon elected William Williams and Joshua West to represent them at the convention. They reaffirmed their faith in non-importation as a virtuous and patriotic means "to procure redress of our Grievances in ye removal of ye unconstitutional duties imposed on America." They considered the conduct of New York alarming and moved that all practical measures should be used "to recover them to their former attachments." They resolved to continue to adhere to the true spirit and meaning of non-importation, and they chose a committee of eight men, headed by Williams, "to observe & inspect ye conduct of all Persons in this Town respecting their violating the true Interest & Meaning of said non-Importation Agree[men]t." In order to further show their devotion to non-importation, the inhabitants called upon Amos Robinson and asked if he had imported tea from Rhode Island contrary to the agreement. Robinson confessed his guilt, but promised not to sell the tea he had on hand. The town deemed his conduct satisfactory and dismissed him. The determination of the inhabitants of Lebanon and the resolutions of the New Haven Convention to continue non-importation until the tax on tea was repealed merited nothing. The boycott on British goods ended.[14]

Politically, the years between 1767 and 1770 saw continued efforts by supporters of Thomas Fitch to recapture the governorship. They directed their efforts first at defeating Governor Pitkin and then at Trumbull, who ascended to the governor's chair upon the death of William Pitkin on October 1, 1769. The Old Lights had made a determined effort as early as 1767 to oust the radicals. Observers then believed that Pitkin would probably be returned to office, since "the Old Lights are not awake yet," but some possibility existed that Silliman and Hamlin, two of the Assistants who had supported Fitch, would "have a Resurrection." Old Light expectations, however slight, proved false, for Pitkin handily defeated Fitch 4,777 to 3,481. Deputy-Governor Trumbull's margin of victory, however, was much smaller. He polled 3,309 votes, compared with 3,039 scattered among various opponents. Trumbull's vote was low because he, much more than Governor Pitkin, was identified with the New Light party. Ebenezer Silliman came within one hundred votes of recapturing his Council seat.[15] Pitkin triumphed over Fitch again in 1768 and 1769, but in 1768 the Old Lights almost succeeded in electing Fitch Chief Judge of the Superior Court in place of Deputy-Governor Trumbull, while in 1769 they tried to secure the Deputy-Governor's post for him after Trumbull failed to receive an electoral majority. Trumbull failed to poll fifty per cent of the votes because, as Williams believed, "our Western Friends especially seem a good deal disaffected." Their professed objection was that the Deputy-Governor did not conduct the business of the Superior Court satisfactorily. The Assembly then narrowly chose Trumbull, but Williams was apprenhensive about the future. The Governor suffered "under ye weight of Age." Conceivably, "a Change may take place another Year."

After the death of the old governor, the Old Lights girded themselves for another effort to return Fitch and expel Trumbull. The election of 1770 was extremely close. Trumbull gained 4,700 votes, Fitch received 4,266 and 805 were scattered. Since the governor failed to secure a majority, the choice again devolved on the legislature, and the Assembly again chose Trumbull.[16] The votes for nomination in September, 1770, reveal the extent of the political split between east and west. Trumbull received 2,930 votes and Fitch 1,979. Trumbull polled 140 votes in Fairfield County, where Fitch gained 607. In Windham County, Trumbull earned 618 votes, Shubael Conant, 778, and William Pitkin, 814, while Fitch received eleven votes, John Chester five, and Ebenezer Sillimain three. At that time, William Williams gained 470 votes, ranking him twenty-eighth among persons nominated for the Council. Williams polled 129 votes in Windham County, but just five in Fairfield County.[17]

The most devisive political issue between 1769 and 1774 was the Susquehannah affair.[18] Organized at Windham in July, 1753, the Susquehannah Company won support from land-hungry farmers and from many of the best-known political figures in the colony, many of them members of the eastern New Light connection. Included among the adherents of western expansion were Eliphalet Dyer, Jedidiah Elderkin, Nathaniel Wales, Jr., and Samuel Gray of Windham, Silas Deane, Matthew Griswold, George Wyllys, General Phineas Lyman, Eleazar Wheelock, and Jonathan Trumbull. In 1754, John Henry Lydius, a Dutch trader of dubious reputation, secured a deed from the Indians to a tract of land along the Susquehanna River in Pennsylvania. Efforts to settle the region aroused the hostility of the Proprietors of Pennsylvania, Sir William Johnson, and Governor Thomas Fitch.

Although efforts were made to distribute shares throughout the colony, the strength of the Susquehannah Company centered in eastern Connecticut. The issue of westward expansion split the colony between east and west and became a factor in the deep hostility between the two sections. A massacre of settlers in 1763, a proclamation by Governor Fitch prohibiting further settlement, and troubles with Britain kept the Susequehannah issue in the background until 1769. But the Treaty of Fort Stanwix, which fixed the Indian boundary west of the Susquehannah territory, set new efforts in motion to establish Connecticut's claim to the territory. The heart of the Susquehannah Company beat in Windham, site of most company meetings and the home of its most enthusiastic supporters, Dyer, Gray, Elderkin, and Wales.[19] Williams, like most persons in Windham County, supported the Company's claims and was a shareholder. But the Susquehannah issue never occupied his attentions to a significant degree, for in only two extant letters prior to 1774 does he mention the matter. He clearly favored, however, Connecticut exploitation of the area.

> I know not what part, if any, the British Ministry will take in the affair, & why shod They, the Lands are doubtless granted & gone from the Crown. They will fill up very much faster under the Tenure of this Colony than any other, & be better defence of this & more advantageous to the mother Country (if She intends we shall Call Her so much longer) & it wod seem very impolitic to favor the exorbitant Claims of the overgrown, overlanded Mr. Penn, & whose Tenants from principle

refuse the use of arms which will probably be yet very necessary on the Borders of ye Savage Country, if not every where else.

Williams also had little good to say about British policy towards the West. The colony bore heavy burdens in the recent war for the sole gain of "avoidance of some trouble with Canada. . . . America fought, America expended . . . immense quantitys of Blood & Treasure . . . & may claim a share in the Honor of Conquest, but G. Britain possesses the whole advantage."[20]

Crucial to the success of the Company, however, were the indefatigable labors in its behalf by Governor Trumbull. The prestige of the Governor's office was expended, and the Company could never have obtained the sanction of the Assembly except for his labors. The crucial vote occurred on October 16, 1773, when the Lower House, which had for four years blocked efforts by the Susquehannah Company to obtain recognition of its claims, resolved to "assert their claim . . . to those lands contained within the limits and boundaries of the charter of this Colony, which are westward of the Province of New York." William Williams, Eliphalet Dyer, Roger Sherman, Matthew Griswold, William Samuel Johnson, Samuel Holden Parsons, Silas Deane, and Jedidiah Strong were appointed to assist the Governor in preparing the claim. Three members were supposed to travel to Pennsylvania and seek an amicable agreement between the two colonies. Williams, Deane, and Strong were included on the committee at the insistence of the Lower House. They had no strong connections with the Company, and they were probably included to offset the partisanship of the Governor.

In November, Trumbull, the available members of the committee, and other interested parties gathered in Norwich to plan the mission and choose the three delegates. Dyer, Johnson, and Strong were ultimately chosen.[21] Williams might have been selected, had it not been for the enmity of Eliphalet Dyer. Williams wrote about the matter in a letter to Dyer, a document which he never sent. He claimed he never wanted to be appointed to the committee and, perhaps protesting too much, stated that he would have refused to go to Philadelphia, even if selected. He knew that if his name were mentioned, Dyer would oppose, but he planned to make no excuse beforehand and allow Dyer "full oppertunity to object." They quickly selected Dyer and Johnson, and Dyer urged that Silas Deane be chosen the third envoy. Deane was objected to because of his business activities. Then Parsons, Strong, and Williams were considered. Parsons declined, and then, without mentioning Williams by name, Dyer proceded to disqualify him by stating that the mission would be best served if all parts of the colony were represented. Johnson lived in Stratford, Dyer in Windham, Williams in the next town, and Strong in Litchfield. The delegates selected Strong, but no other person present, according to Williams, "thot it of any importance to have ye Comtee scattered into different parts of ye Colony." Williams realized that Dyer had long harbored "a bitterness of Spirit & implacable Disposition towards" him, but he claimed there was no reason for it. He sardonically thanked Dyer for his efforts, but not for his motives.[22] The delegates travelled to Philadelphia, but all efforts to reach an accommodation failed, and the Assembly, in special session in January, 1774, resolved to extend its jurisdiction over the Susquehannah territory. The inhabitants were constituted into a distinct town called Westmoreland, and the new town was annexed to Litchfield County.[23]

The last effort by anti-Susquehannah supporters of Governor Fitch to regain control of the colony came in 1774. The radicals triumphed, and in July, Thomas Fitch, the conservative leader, died. The defeat of the conservatives in 1774, in a campaign waged largely on Susquehannah, meant far more than approval of western expansion. "For that defeat ensured Whig control of the provincial government during the grave months when the colonies were to be engaged in their last controversy with Britain."[24]

*

After 1766, Williams' political star continued to rise. He was Clerk of the House, Major of the Twelfth Militia Regiment, and served on numerous committees. The Assembly appointed him one of four Justices of the Peace and Quorum for Windham County in May, 1769. Three years later, he became lieutenant colonel of the Twelfth Regiment and was promoted to colonel in May, 1775. In May, 1774, he was temporarily chosen Speaker to replace Ebenezer Silliman, who was called home because of sickness in the family. The Assembly elected him Speaker in October. Williams was first nominated to the Chamber of Assistants in October, 1774, when he ranked twentieth and last in the list of nominees. The following year he rose to fifteenth and polled 2,875 votes. In May, 1776, he took a seat on the Council. The legislature appointed him Judge of the Court of Probate for the Windham district in May, 1775, to replace Shubael Conant of Mansfield, and in October, after Conant's death, he was appointed Judge of the Windham County Court.[25]

Plural officeholding was common in eighteenth-century Connecticut. By independence, Williams had engrossed almost every position of authority that a man could acquire in Lebanon, Windham County, and Connecticut. This pattern of multiple officeholding was duplicated by other political leaders in the colony. A man's reputation was not normally based on any single office, but on their quantity and quality. A political career commenced with service to the town. Political horizons expanded with election to the Assembly. The legislature chose militia officers, Justices, Judges of Probate, County Court Judges, and committees. Once a man became a Justice and served on committees, he could gain the further esteem of his peers, gain a reputation beyond the borders of his hometown, and the path of the able, fortunate, and respected to still higher positions opened. Only a few, however, reached the Council, a position that was normally the pinnacle of a political career in colonial Connecticut. The success of William Williams was due in large measure to his leadership in the New Light faction. Conceivably, though certainly not so quickly, Williams could have attained equal reputation had not political habits in Connecticut been so unsteady, but his position and influence in the colony was a direct consequence of his activity in behalf of the eastern party.

*

The repercussions from the *Gaspee* affair and reports that the salaries of Superior Court judges and the governor in Massachusetts would henceforth be drawn from customs revenues had led to the formation in November, 1772, of the Boston Committee of Correspondence. Far sighted radicals in the Lower House established Connecticut's Committee of Correspondence on May 21, 1773. The committee was charged to obtain intelligence and maintain correspondence with their sister colonies respecting the securing of America's legal and constitutional rights. The committee consisted of nine members, seven radicals and two moderates. The Seven Sons of Liberty members were William Williams, Samuel Holden Parsons, Silas Deane, Benjamin Payne, Nathaniel Wales, Samuel Bishop, and Joseph Trumbull. The two moderates were Ebenezer Silliman and Erastus Wolcott. Although most Connecticut patriots were preoccupied with the Susquehannah affair, the committee was soon engaged in trying to discover suspected enemies of liberty and was corresponding with committees in other colonies.[26] A letter written by Williams on August 10, 1773, and signed by Williams, Deane, Payne, and Trumbull and addressed to the Virginia Committee of Correspondence, informed the Virginia patriots that Connecticut had constituted a committee of correspondence in accordance with the proposal of the Virginians, told of the goings on in Rhode Island respecting investigation of the *Gaspee* incident, and concluded with the hope that the committees would strengthen the harmony and union of the English colonies.[27]

The Tea Act of 1773 precipitated the final crisis. The financially-troubled East India Company was allowed for the first time to import tea directly to America free of all English taxes except the Townshend duty. These privileges enabled the Company to undersell smuggled tea and control the colonial market. Americans objected because a powerful tea monopoly had been created, and because inexpensive tea was seen as a trap to induce them to accept Parliamentary taxation.

Patriots compelled vessels carrying consignments of tea to return to England. Governor Hutchinson, however, refused to allow the laden ships to return, and the Bostonians responded on the night of December 16, 1773, by pitching the tea into Boston harbor. An incensed British government resolved to punish Boston in order to demonstrate that Parliament was supreme. The government enacted four bills designed to punish the city, the so-called Coercive Acts. Connecticut Patriots, in the midst of the last act of the Susquehannah struggle, paid little attention to the Tea Act until after the Boston Tea Party occurred. In March, 1774, however, the Committee of Correspondence noted that no news from Britain had been received. They still lacked any knowledge of Britain's intentions respecting the destruction of tea in Boston and the return of tea from other ports.[28]

After opponents of Susquehannah were soundly defeated in 1774, Susquehannah disappeared as a political issue, and patriots focused on the tragic news from Boston. The Lower House approved a statement in May which condemned the Coercive Acts for the penalties they inflicted on a city that had so ardently defended America's liberties, but the more cautious Upper House delayed approval of the resolutions until October. The report affirmed that Americans had the right to enjoy all the liberties of English-born subjects who could not be rightfully taxed except by their own consent. It condemned the Intolerable Acts for being contrary to Connecticut's sacred charter and proclaimed that Parliament, in closing the Port of Boston, had set a precedent that was "justly alarming to the British Colonies in America, and wholly inconsistent with and subversive of their constitutional rights and liberties." The Assembly also recommended that the people observe a day of public fasting and prayer to protest British actions. In addition, the Assembly urged the towns to contribute to the relief of the poor in Boston, an act which the legislature twice reaffirmed. On June 3, the Lower House empowered the Committee of Correspondence to choose delegates to attend a Congress of the British colonies in North America.[29]

During the spring and summer, towns throughout the colony, and and in Windham County in particular, adopted manifestoes supporting Boston, condemning the Coercive Acts, calling for an intercontinental Congress, establishing local committees of correspondence, and demanding the establishment of non-importation agreements.[30] June 1, 1774, the date "on which the cruel Edict of the British Parliament respecting . . . Boston took place," was observed in Lebanon as a day of mourning. In the evening, the elderly Whig pastor, Solomon Williams, proclaimed that the time had come "to determine whether we will tamely submit to every Act of cruel Oppression or indignantly reject . . . every instance of unjust power." The minister introduced, and the town unanimously adopted, declarations affirming their hearty sympathy with their brethren in Boston, pledging their support of whatever measures were deemed necessary to secure America's liberties, and affirming that the cause of Boston, "suffering under the hand of ministerial vengeance," was the cause of liberty and the common cause of mankind.[31]

Williams was deeply engaged in the summer of 1774 in stirring up enthusiasm for the Patriot cause. He wrote two letters published in the *Connecticut Gazette* in July, took the lead in stirring up resistance to Britain in Lebanon, and was intensely involved in the activities of the Committee of Correspondence. On July 1, the *Gazette* published an address "To the King" signed "America." In this long document, Williams castigated the king for shutting his eyes and ears to America's complaints.

> We don't complain that your father made our yoke heavy and afflicted us with grievous service. We only ask that you would govern us upon the same constitutional plan, and with the same justice and moderation that he did, and we will serve you forever. And what is the language of your answer . . . ? Ye Rebels and Traitors . . . if ye don't yield implicit obedience to all my commands, just and unjust, ye shall be drag'd in chains across the wide ocean, to answer your insolence, and if a mob arises among you to impede my officers in the execution of my orders, I will punish and involve in common ruin whole cities and colonies, with their ten thousand innocents, and ye shan't be heard in your own defense, but shall be murdered and butchered by my dragoons into silence and submission. Ye reptiles! ye are scarce intitled to existence any longer. . . . Your lives, liberties and property are all at the absolute disposal of my parliament.

He reminded the king that Englishmen had always hated slavery and that the fathers of New England had fled from tyranny and oppression in order to enjoy the sacred rights of Englishmen. "But you have conceived Sir, most ungrounded prejudices against your faithful Americans," and thus have almost totally alienated the affection of the American colonies. Americans were zealously and unalterably attached to their constitutional rights and liberties "to which we were born, and in possession of which we are resolved to die."[32] The next week, under the pseudonym "Cato Americanus," Colonel Williams addressed the inhabitants of Boston. The entire continent proclaimed the cause of Boston to be the common cause. Hopefully, they would convince Britain that it was "infinite madness to destroy themselves [and] to enslave us." They may effect the former, but never the latter. The liberties of the nation were too sacred to be parted with under any terms. "If it cost us but half our estates to secure our liberties, the remainder will be much better than the whole by so wretched a tenure as present."[33]

On July 18, three hundred citizens in Lebanon gathered to consider the alarming situation. Directed by Moderator Williams, the inhabitants declared that the recent acts of Parliament represented "an

Axe laid to the Root of the Tree and in direct Opposition to and utterly subversive of this and every Claim and Idea of Liberty and Property in English America." They considered the cause of Boston to be the cause of America, and they affirmed that, if Congress should agree to break off all commercial intercourse with Britain until American liberties were restored, they would gladly adhere to such an agreement. They appointed William Williams, Jonathan Trumbull, Jr., Joshua West, and three others a committee of correspondence, and they affirmed that it was the duty of every inhabitant to contribute to aid the suffering citizens of Boston.[34]

As early as June 3, the townspeople had collected money to help the Boston poor, but on August 8, the town, prodded by the Selectmen, sent three hundred and seventy-six "fat sheep for the relief of those who are most unable to support themselves." On October 3, the remaining portion of the collection, beef cattle worth £30, was dispatched to Boston. Williams assured the Bostonians that the people of the town "greatly applaud your firmness and resolution." A further effort to aid the Bostonians was made on April 24, 1775.[35]

At meetings on July 13 and August 3, 1774, the Committee of Correspondence selected three delegates to attend the First Continental Congress: Silas Deane, Eliphalet Dyer, and Roger Sherman. Williams hoped that Congress would recommend the immediate breaking off of commercial intercourse with Britain. If America did not have enough virtue to do so, he did not think the colonies would have sufficient virtue "to take up Arms & Shed rivers of Blood in defense of our most infinitely important Cause." He also distrusted Silas Deane.[36] He warned Sam Adams that "Mr. D" was "not genuine." His persuasiveness, and the West Indian interest, secured Deane's election by one vote, but Williams so mistrusted him that "I my Self got him Cler of our Correspond[enc]e."[37] Deane, he was afraid, would try to use his considerable powers of persuasion to prevent breaking off the West Indian trade.[38]

At this critical juncture, the position of outspoken Tories became intolerable. Windham Patriots drove Francis Green, a well-known Boston adherent of General Cage, out of town on July 4, 1774, and radicals from Lebanon and Windham took the lead in forcing the notorious Anglican clergyman, Samuel Peters, to flee Hebron in September.[39] The Sons of Liberty visited the unhappy cleric on August 14 and September 6 and threatened to return again. Peters appealed vainly for protection from Governor Trumbull and then fled to Boston. One can almost see the fine hand of Patriots, like Colonel Williams, behind the attacks on Peters. In any case, Williams accurately summed up Patriot sentiments about the affair. The people had treated Peters "with much more decency than is common for mobs." Although Williams deplored the mob's behavior, Peters had long been suspected of harboring "sentiments inimical" to his native country, and Williams had heard that Peters was planning to go to England, filled with "evil and false representations" about the colonies. No government has ever been entirely free of such disturbances, he wrote, but Connecticut "has had less of the them than perhaps any in the world."[40]

Connecticut moved steadily and unrelentingly towards revolution. On September 3, a report spread to the colony that British troops had fired on the citizens of Boston. The rumor proved false, but before that was known, thousands had begun to march to Massachusetts.[41] On September 8, 1774, Whigs from eighteen towns in Windham and New London Counties met in convention in Norwich "to consult for their common safety." Gurdon Saltonstall of New London chaired the convention and Colonel William Williams served as Clerk. The convention, "taking into their serious Consideration the present State of this Country," advised the Selectmen and militia officers of each town to increase their stock of military stores and to see that all troops had proper equipment. It also recommended that additional training be provided for all militiamen and that each regiment stage a military review. The delegates also petitioned the General Assembly. They feared they would soon be faced with the "disagreeable Necessity of defending our sacred & invaluable Rights, sword in hand," because they did not believe that any true American "possibly could be dragooned into Slavery." They urged, therefore, that the militia laws be revised in order to put the forces on a "more respectable footing." The town representatives sent a similar letter to Connecticut's delegates in the Continental Congress. A week later, a convention of delegates from Hartford, New London, Windham, and Litchfield Counties met in Hartford. They proclaimed the absolute necessity for a non-importation and non-consumption agreement and, since some mercenary wretches had engrossed excessively large quantities of English goods, they directed local committees of correspondence to seek out and refuse to do business with such men.[42]

In October, 1774, the Lower House elected William Williams to the post of Speaker, and then immediately took up the militia question, as recommended by the Norwich Convention. The first statute passed provided for the encouragement of military training and defense. Another act doubled the quantity of powder, ball, and flints in town stocks, while another stipulated that proper carriages for the cannon at New London be secured. Governor Trumbull believed that the colony had better prepare for the storm, and the Speaker agreed. "Things look serious respect[in]g our Liberties, a large Com[mit]tee is out considering Militia Matters."[43] Congress at Philadelphia recommended the establishment of continental machinery for resistance. During the late fall and winter, Connecticut towns ratified the recommendations of Congress and set up committees to enforce the Continental Association. The inhabitants of Lebanon, on December 12, endorsed the recommendations of Congress relative to non-importation and non-consumption of British goods, a non-exportation agreement, and the need to promote domestic manufactures. They also selected a "Committee of Inspection or Safety" to "observe the Conduct of all Persons in the Town touching said Association." The committee consisted of twelve men, including William Williams, Joshua West, Jonathan Trumbull, Jr., and Vetch Williams. By the beginning of 1775, Williams, speaking for the Connecticut Committee of Correspondence, could report with satisfaction "that the People of this Colony are more & more united, the Scales seem to fall from the Eyes of our western Bretheren." The union of the colonies in adopting the resolves of Congress was "surprizing & glorious."[44]

To supplement local committees of inspection, Patriots organized county conventions to draw up provisions for enforcing the Continental Association. The Windham County Convention, chaired by Joshua West of Lebanon, on February 16, 1775, ordered merchants to reduce their trade in English goods as soon as possible and sell them at reasonable prices. To prevent the engrossment of unnecessarily large quanities of British goods by "ill-minded Traders," the Convention directed that no English goods be sold or brought into the county until the retailer procurred an invoice from the local committee of inspection that the products were necessary for the welfare of the people. Any person found guilty of violating the Association would be "proceeded against, treated, and exposed as an Enemy to this injured Country." The Convention advised the people to prepare for battle, "prepare for the worst . . . expect shortly to meet the Enemy in the Gate." They were enjoined to lay aside controversies and to remember "that your Union (under God) is your sure Bulwark."[45]

As the crisis deepened, Connecticut Patriots resolved to use the full weight of the colonial government against their political foes. They planned for the "last Extremity," and, due to their influence, a special session of the legislature was called for March 2, 1775. The Assembly ordered investigations of militia officers accused of Toryism and established a committee to examine affairs in the Tory towns of Ridgefield and Newtown. The members well understood the gravity of the situation. The Lower House again urged the citizens of Connecticut to come to the aid of Boston and directed the Speaker to write to the Speaker of the House in Jamaica to thank that body for its support of the mainland colonies. Williams, after praising the Jamaicans for acknowledging the justice of the colonial position, asserted that the colonies, "by the unwearied efforts of our enemies," have been brought "near to a most alarming crisis." The colonies were threatened by the "dreadful alternative of surrendering all for which our fathers suffered and bled, all that is deserving of men, Englishmen and Americans . . .

or suffer all the horrours of a military contention with the Parent State." But the unity of the colonies, the justice of their cause, and the approbation of their fellowmen gave them support and consolation.[46]

Connecticut was virtually at a state of war even before Lexington and Concord. The colony had rejected Parliament's authority to tax its residents, was taking steps to suppress Tories, and was prepared to fight to uphold its rights and liberties. Although in a letter to the Earl of Dartmouth, they reaffirmed their loyalty to the crown, at the same time they voted not to petition the king because, as Williams stated, "so many have been rejected by the Influence of evil Councillors, that we have little reason to expect another wod fare any better." Speaker Williams and other Patriots continually emphasized that they were firmly resolved to defend their constitutional liberties. "But should violence essay to enslave them, they believe they are warranted by the example of Great Britain and the Constitution itself, to defend themselves, and repel any lawless invasion."[47]

In the month before the outbreak of fighting, Williams, under the pseudonyms of "Amicus Patriae" and "Americanus," addressed Connecticut Patriots. He condemned "the Paracides of their Country," who were "straining every Nerve . . . to aid the excerable Plan of exterminating Liberty from the face of the Earth by enslaving America." He rejoiced, therefore, that the "Colony is firm almost without an exception" in a determination to defend America's liberties, for in the recent meeting of the General Assembly there occurred "very little difference of Sentiment save only as to timeing of Measures." Two weeks before Lexington, Colonel Williams urged that militia regiments in the region schedule their exercises on the same day.[48] Williams was virtually certain that civil war would ensue, and thus he used his considerable powers to awaken the populace and persuade the Assembly to prepare for the worst. For over six months he preached this message and, when first shots were fired, few in Connecticut were surprised and most were prepared to resist.

Fighting erupted on April 19, 1775. Once the news reached Connecticut, men from forty-nine Connecticut towns marched on Boston and a special session of the legislature was called for April 26. The Committee of Correspondence informed John Hancock on April 21 that the colony was preparing to help their brothers in Massachusetts. "The ardour of our people is such, that they can't be kept back." The day after the legislature convened, Speaker Williams reported to his Lebanon constituents that, although he could not report particulars because the members took an oath of secrecy, "the unnatural sheding the Blood of our dear Countrymen seems to have had a wonderfull Effect to unite all in great Resolution to defend & avenge innocent blood." He believed that the Assembly "shall do all You & I Wish, & that is saying a good deal." He also recommended that the town's flints be removed from the town house, that additional supplies of powder be acquired, and that the repairing of guns "be pursued with the very utmost & unremitting Zeal & activity." They cannot subdue America, he vowed, and concluded, "We are determined to stand fast."[49] The legislature acted decisively. The Assembly laid an embargo on the export of provisions, directed that one quarter of the militia be organized and equipped "for the special defense and safety of the Colony," appointed Joseph Trumbull Commissary General, voted to print £50,000 in paper money, and appointed overseers of powder and cannon. They also urged the ministers to dissuade their congregations from all excesses, and appealed to them to "cry mightily to God, that he would be pleased to spare his people."[50]

On April 26, in response to reports that the Americans had been the aggressors and had begun the battle, Williams, speaking for the majority in the Lower House, affirmed that one thousand British troops had marched to Lexington, where they found about fifty Americans "collected for Military Exercise without any Knoledge that Soldiers were near them." The British accosted them, harangued them with profane language, and ordered them to disperse. As they were obeying, "the Kings Troops fired upon Them . . . & killed 8 Men on the Spot." How, Williams asked, could one believe that a handful of men "wod expose Themselves to certain Death by beginning a Fire on such a Body of well armed Troops?" Thus it is declared by every voice that the King's men commenced firing. The Assembly "is firmly persuaded that this is the Truth & it is earnestly requested That if any of the Nation doubts, They will suspend Their Belief, till Evidence be received which shall convince every rational Mind" that the British fired first. As soon as such conclusive evidence was received, the Assembly would transmit it, but at present it was impossible to discover the total truth.[51]

Despite making all these preparations for war, the legislature, on April 28, 1775, moved seemingly in the opposite direction. In a step that embarrassed and confused loyal Whigs, the Assembly decided to send William Samuel Johnson and Erastus Wolcott, both conservatives, on a special mission to General Gage. They carried a letter from Governor Trumbull in which he warned Gage that Connecticut would not remain as spectators should the horrors of civil war ensue, adding, "is there no way to prevent this unhappy dispute from coming to extremities?" Trumbull asked the general for further information, requested him to explain his intentions, and concluded with the hope that a last-minute compromise might yet avert war. The letter and the mission of the two conservatives aroused great anxiety among Patriots in Massachusetts and the Connecticut troops there. It is conceivable that Governor Trumbull, Speaker Williams, and other sturdy Patriots may have suddenly gotten cold feet, although the evidence does not support such a conclusion.

Three separate motives induced the Assembly to support the embassy. The legislature still included a handful of Tories and a larger number of moderates who welcomed the mission. Many good Whigs considered the maneuver a means to clearly fix the responsibiilty for the first battle on the British, and others considered it a strategic expedient to gain time for additional military preparations. In any case, the mission failed. Before Johnson and Wolcott returned with Gage's conciliatory reply, the Assembly had adjourned and Gage's letter was ignored. By September, 1775, the general had concluded that the mission had been conceived in "Treachery and Deceit."[52]

The Speaker supported the embassy as an expedient for gaining time and, secondarily, as a means of ascertaining more conclusively the responsibility for Lexington and Concord. On May 1, 1775, he reassured Joseph Trumbull that the Connecticut legislature was "not asleep nor unmindfull of ye grand Cause." He warned that since Gage had not yet attacked the besieging New England forces, danger existed that they would become too confident and Gage would have the opportunity to strike. Moreover, Connecticut needed further evidence of Gage's first attack or many would believe his witnesses. Williams concluded with a recommendation not to attack.

> I am firmly persuaded [he wrote] tis not best to attack [Gage] in his Intrench[me]nts, but ye proper Moment shod not be neglected. Tis said ye present Struggle is of so desperate a Temper yt We are neither to expect nor give quarter, yt whatever blow is struck shod from its magnitude & violence be worth [of] ye Dignity & desparation of ye Cause.

Three days later, in order to reassure Massachusetts, Williams affirmed that the legislature loyally supported the noble cause. The embassy of Johnson and Wolcott was prompted by a concern that an immediate attack on an intrenched General Gage "without a moral certainty of Success & without great Consideration might not be prudent." It was still possible, though not probable, that "further Extremity" might be avoided, and, more importantly, "We conceived that You & We might get more advantage by gaining Time & collecting all our Forces." Volunteers could be gathered under a regular plan. Still, the embassy proved embarrassing, and by May 6, Williams hoped that the mission would have no permanent ill effects. As for the commissioners, Johnson was "amazingly fearful" of the power of Britain, while Wolcott could probably be trusted, although he "was slow & very cautious."[53]

The special session adjourned on May 5, and the regular session convened on May 11. The legislature resolutely embarked on further preparations for conflict. They despatched four regiments to Massachusetts, adopted official articles of war, extended the embargo, voted to print another £50,000 of paper money, cashiered three Tory militia officers, passed a law encouraging the manufacture of military supplies, and created a Council of Safety to assist the Governor.[54] Speaker Williams was one of seven persons appointed to procure firearms and encourage their manufacture and was one of nine persons selected for the Council of Safety. The Assembly also chose him Judge of the Court of Probate for the Windham district to replace the ailing Shubael Conant and appointed him colonel of the Twelfth Regiment in the room of Joseph Spencer, who had been chosen brigadier general of Connecticut forces in Massachusetts.[55] As Speaker, Williams engaged in all the important acts of the Assembly and had no doubts about the direction in which Connecticut was moving.

> Grand Events will take Place, what ye Result [will be] God only knows. We hope ye best, let every one cry with redoubled ardor to Him who can with infinite Ease blast ye Designs of our Enemies, & repent & reform so We may hope [for] a happy Issue.[56]

✿

During the war, Williams devoted most of his time and energy to the Council of Safety, an organization that superseded the Committee of Correspondence. The Assembly charged the Council to assist the Governor in directing the war effort when the Assembly was not in session. The original Council consisted of nine men, all from eastern Connecticut. In addition to Deputy-Governor Matthew Griswold of Lyme, the committee included three Assistants and five present or former members of the Lower House. Except for the Deputy-Governor, all members chosen resided in either Lebanon, Windham, or Norwich, the purpose being to lessen travel costs. Trumbull, Williams, and Joshua West lived in Lebanon; Eliphalet Dyer, Jedidiah Elderkin, and Nathaniel Wales, Jr., lived in Windham; and Jabez, Samuel, and Benjamin Huntington were from Norwich. The Council of Safety's size increased as the war lengthened. The Assembly chose ten persons in 1776, fourteen in 1777, and an average of twenty a year from 1778 through 1783. Forty-four persons served on the Council in its eight and a half year existence. Fifteen served at least four years, but only Deputy-Governor Griswold and Williams were chosen every year.[57] At first the members came from eastern Connecticut, but prominent politicians from central and western Connecticut later became members, persons like Roger Sherman, Abraham Davenport, William Pitkin, Benjamin Payne, Joseph Platt Cook, Jedidiah Strong, and Oliver Wolcott. According to the author's count, the Council of Safety held 1,002 meetings, 556 in the Governor's home town of Lebanon. Four hundred and five meetings were held in Hartford and the remaining forty-one in six other communities. Except for the Governor, William Williams probably attended more meetings than anyone else. He was present at 622.[58] At the first meeting on June 7, 1775, the Council elected Williams

Clerk, a position he retained as long as the organization existed. When he was absent, James Wadsworth, Jesse Root, or Benjamin Payne replaced him. He served without pay, and by November, 1782, his financial position was so poor that he petitioned the Council for assistance. During his long term of service, he had "drafted, recorded & copied many hundred acts & resolves" without receiving "one farthing of reward therefor directly or indirectly & being now in want of some Salt for his Family use," he prayed to be granted three bushels of rock salt. The Council granted the memorial.[59]

The Council of Safety was given full power and authority to order and direct the militia and naval forces of the colony. It had the power to send troops to help defend other colonies and oversee the furnishing of Connecticut's forces "in every respect and to every purpose that may be needful to render the defense of these Colonies effectual." Williams' activties were primarily clerical, but on occasions he undertook other duties. On July 13, 1775, Williams and Samuel Huntington were delegated to confer with a disgruntled General Spencer, who threatened to resign his commission after Congress made Israel Putnam a major general, while Spencer, an older man of higher rank in the militia, was made a brigadier general. Huntington and Williams managed to "reconcile him chearfully to pursue the service."[60] On July 24, Williams, Wales, and two others were appointed to find two armed vessels for the defense of the colony. The Council also directed them to examine cannon at New Haven and give directions for preparing gun carriages for them. On August 2, the Council resolved to take over a 108-ton brig belonging to Captain William Griswold of Wethersfield and charter a smaller vessel for spy purposes. On September 8, the Council gave Williams and Wales a particularly important mission to execute. The Second Continental Congress decided that war burdens should be jointly shared, and, at the same time, voted to reimburse Connecticut for her war expenses. Williams and Wales were delegated to go to Philadelphia to obtain the money. They left on September 18 and arrived there on September 26. On September 27, 1775, Congress voted to pay Connecticut 160,000 dollars. On March 14, 1776, the Council chose Williams and Eliphalet Dyer "to repair to Philadelphia [and] apply to Continental Congress for a remittance of continental bills" due the colony. They were also supposed to examine the circumstances of two regiments of Connecticut troops in New York, ask the Yorkers for a loan of cannon, and confer with the delegates at Congress on "matters relative to the state of the United Colonies." They set out on March 25, reached Philadelphia on April 4, conferred with the delegates, began the journey home on April 18, turned over 166,666 dollars to Treasurer John Lawrence on April 26, and reached Lebanon the next day.[61]

*

Another special session of the Assembly was held in July, 1775. Two additional regiments were raised and sent to Massachusetts, and another £50,000 in colony paper was printed to cover the increasing military costs. Williams reported with satisfaction that the Assembly was "almost to a Man deeply impressed with the highest Sense of Importance of supporting at every Hazard and Expence, a Cause unspeakably important and big with the Fate of born and unborn Millions." He was pleased with the union of the colonies and affirmed that "one half of our Estates will be deemed a small Sacrifice in a Cause of such magnitude."[62]

Military preparations continued to dominate the affairs of the Assembly at the regular October session and the special December session of the legislature, while Williams' political star continued to rise. Williams ranked fifteenth on the nominations list in October, and the Assembly chose him Judge of the Windham County Court to replace the deceased Shubael Conant. The Assembly also elected new delegates to Congress. They recalled Silas Deane and Eliphalet Dyer, reelected Roger Sherman, chose Oliver Wolcott and Samuel Huntington to replace the two deposed delegates, and appointed William Williams and Titus Hosmer as alternates. [63]

The removal of Deane and Dyer was justified by the principle of rotation, but personal animosities and conflicting political ambitions had developed among leading members of the popular party. The relationship between Williams and Dyer was chilly, while Williams and Deane despised each other. Deane and Sherman disliked one another, and Dyer had enemies in eastern Connecticut. Deane deeply resented the designs of his enemies to supersede him, and he correctly identified the efforts as the work of a junto headed by Speaker Williams. Deane's "true friends found the junto had levied their artilery" against him and had secured "a large majority of the present members in favor of both Col. Dyer & you being recalled." Deane blamed Williams in particular for his fall from grace, "that little malevolent prig in buckram" who led the party men in his neighborhood. Deane had many other enemies in the Patriot party in New Haven and Fairfield Counties, but Williams played a crucial role in censuring him and checkmating his political career in Connecticut.[64]

In December, the legislature passed its first comprehensive measure against the Tories. Persons convicted of aiding the enemy could be imprisoned and have their estates forfeited, while persons who spoke against Congress or the Assembly lost all political privileges. Town officers had the authority to examine suspected persons and disarm them. The situation was unusual. Connecticut was still a British colony, but her authorities had declared that it was illegal to be loyal to Britain.[65]

Throughout the war, Williams' labors were prodigious, and, although he possessed a strong constitution, his health suffered by unremitting application to duty. By early 1776, the council of Safety averaged three meetings a week, and Williams complained: "You can not think nor conceve the unremitting Applications to the Govr about a thousand things in this pressing critical Time, which creates much business for ye Council." Williams' mercantile business ended as he resolved to devote all his energies to the struggle against Britain. In March, 1776, he endeavored to collect potash, but said he could afford to pay no more than four and a half pence per bushel, because "I am out of any Business of Profit to get a Living by." The specie he possessed he exchanged for paper, hoping thereby to halt inflation. The money was lost, but if the colonies were defeated, it would not matter anyway, because he expected to hang.[66] He welcomed passing soldiers at his home and collected one thousand blankets and large supplies of lead, clothing, and foodstuffs for Connecticut's troops.[67]

By the spring of 1776, independence sentiment was strong in Connecticut, although the Assembly in its regular May session did not instruct its delegates to vote for independence. When Dyer and Williams travelled to Philadelphia in April, they discussed the matter with the other delegates, but they were unable to find sufficient independence sentiment to get action from the legislature. But towards the close of the session, the Assembly issued a ringing declaration emphasizing the critical situation and the justice of American resistance. The colonies were threatened by the whole force of Great Britain, aided by German mercenaries. These troops were engaged in spreading murder, rapine, and destruction. "In this situation our utmost efforts cannot be too much, and it is the duty of every individual to contribute all in his power to serve and defend our most important cause." The legislature occupied itself with military preparations, for though Boston had been evacuated, a British attack on New York was expected, and the colonies had already met defeat in Canada. The unhappy news from the north, however, must not dishearten America. "We must think," Williams stated, "our Cause is just & that God will yet appear for Us, however, the utmost Attention and vigilence is necessary."[68]

At the same session, William Williams and Richard Law of New London were elevated to the Chamber of Assistants to replace conservative William Samuel Johnson and the deceased Shubael Conant.[69]

Scarcely had the regular session adjourned, however, when, on urgent request from Congress, a special session was called for June 14. Congress wanted Connecticut to furnish 1,500 additional men for Canada and 5,500 to reinforce New York. This was done, but, more importantly, Connecticut voted to instruct her delegates in Congress to vote for independence. The Lower House unanimously resolved on June 14, 1776:

That the Delegates of this Colony in General Congress be and they are hereby instructed to propose to that respectable body, to declare the United American Colonies Free and Independent States, absolved from all allegiance to the King of Great Britain.

Three men chosen by the Upper House, including William Williams, met with a committee chosen by the Lower House to consider the propriety of the resolution. The instructions received the approbation of the Council on the morning of June 15, 1776. Three days later, Governor Trumbull issued a proclamation, written by Williams, in which he eloquently described the principles for which they were fighting. The proclamation concluded with a forceful plea for God's aid:

> Let every one to the utmost of their Power lend a helping Hand to promote and forward a Design on which the Salvation of America now evidently depends. . . . I do hereby earnestly recommend it to all . . . frequently to meet together for social Prayer to ALMIGHTY GOD, for the out-pouring of his blessed Spirit upon this guilty Land—That he would awaken his People to Rightousness and Repentence—bless our Councils—prosper our Arms, and succeed the Measures using for our necessary Self-Defense.[70]

Williams and the overwhelming majority of the people in Connecticut moved towards independence with few regrets. Indeed, many of the acts between October, 1775, and May, 1776, that mobilized the colony for war and moved Connecticut towards independence were drafted by Williams. As Williams phrased it, if the American cause required "the last farthing I have, She is double welcome, tis much better expended than to support the Tyrant Lords who will succeed the Loss of Liberty.[71]

*

William Williams' interpretation of the American Revolution should not seem unusual to those acquainted with the rhetoric of the period. He deeply believed that Americans were entitled to all the rights of Englishmen and that British actions after 1763 represented an unconstitutional abridgement of America's liberties. He also, being an extremely devout man, expressed the conviction that America could hope and trust that God would grant the nation salvation. Thirdly, considerable evidence exists to support the hypothesis of Bernard Bailyn that Americans feared that the British were conspiring to destroy American liberty.

The colonists firmly believed that British efforts to tax them were an unconstitutional infringement of American liberty. Williams viewed the Townshend Act, levied "for the purpose of raising a Revenue . . . in no other Light than the Stamp Dutys." He affirmed that the "Rights & Liberties of ye Country" were more sacred than life, and that the Townshend Acts "grant away our property without our consent" and thus "unhinge the British constitution and sap the foundations of

American liberty." Americans were "most zealously and unalterably attached to our constitutional Rights and Liberties to which we were born, and in possession of which we are resolved to die." The colonists, Williams declared, had the unshaken belief that they could claim "all the Rights, Immunities, and Privileges of free and natural English Subjects." The Coercive Acts, he stated, were utterly subversive to "every Claim and Idea of Liberty and Property in English America."[72]

Americans, particularly those of an evangelical persuasion, increasingly began to invoke the aid of God as war drew ever closer. On June 1, 1774, the townspeople of Lebanon prayed that God, "the Great Father of the distressed," would direct America's councils. "Cato Americanus" optimistically believed that Americans would "see the salvation of our God in the success of our efforts." Williams trusted that God was on America's side. "The Cause of Liberty is the Cause of God." He would not abandon America nor forsake those who trusted Him. Once fighting commenced, his optimism lessened. On May 1, 1775, he wrote, "We are not dismayed" but put "our trust in ye God of Hosts, & relying on his infinite Mercy to support us in so just a Cause." "We humbly Hope That Heaven will approve and smile propitious on our common Attempts to vindicate the Rights and Liberties which God almighty gave to be the common Lot and Portion of Mankind." Sometimes a dual theme was expressed. America's trials were caused by her sinfulness, but America could hope and trust in God's mercy. "Let every one repent & cry out to Heaven with ten fold more ardor than Ninevah, tho much is to be feared, nothing is to be dispaired." The colonists must trust that God will not forsake them, "tho' our Iniquities testify against us, yet trusting in his Mercy, we believe it to be his command, and our indispensable Duty to Him, to Ourselves and Posterity, to stand fast" to maintain the liberty which God gave America.[73]

Bernard Bailyn has persuasively argued that the leaders of the Revolutionary movement viewed English policy after 1763 as a conspiracy on the part of evil men within the government to overthrow the British constitution and destroy American liberty. Americans constantly reiterated the conviction that Britain aimed to enslave them. In January, 1770, Williams emphasized that strict adherence to the nonimportation agreements was necessary to save the country from oppression "tending to end in full & compleat Slavery." "Cato Americanus" insisted that British measures aimed at accomplishing the slavery of America. The present ministry wished to reduce the colonies to "miserable bondage." Conspirators within the British government were deemed responsible for the effort to destroy America's liberties. Their distresses were the "consequence of measures planned by a few artful, designing men." The Coercive Acts were the consequence "of ministerial vengeance" for the noble exertions of the people of Boston in the cause of liberty. Williams emphasized that the king had been induced by lies and slanders to proclaim that the liberty, property, and lives of Americans were at his absolute disposal. The Tories, too, were involved in the conspiracy. Williams accused the Loyalists, "the Paracides of their Country," of straining every nerve "to aid the execrable Plan of exterminating Liberty from the face of the Earth by enslaving America."[74]

Williams penned his most complete view of British aims after fighting broke out. The struggle in which America was engaged was fraught "with Consequences the most Weighty that ever effected this Country or any of the Race of Mankind." The issue was whether Americans "shall any longer enjoy the Sweets of Virtuous Liberty," or whether they would "become the tributary Slaves & Vassals of haughty Masters," and have "our Houses burnt, our Lands . . . wrested from Us & possessed by petty impotent Tyrants, our Wives & Daughters ravished at their brutal Pleasure," and our little children "dashed against the stones." All this "to support in Riot, affluence, & Grandeur a ruthless Train of the most idle, profane, dissolute, & worthless Wretches that ever disgraced Humanity." This was "no Runt of Fancy," but was "the determined Plan of our Enemies," the "cunning & malicious Administration of ye Kingdom of Great Britain, supported by the delegated Power of its Supreme Legislature."[75] Such powerful, dramatic, and picturesque language came from deep conviction, and Williams' pen was a powerful weapon in Connecticut's patriot armor.

The Years of War

WILLIAM WILLIAMS is best known as a signer of the Declaration of Independence. But Williams only served reluctantly in Congress, although he conscientiously represented the interests of his native state. A delegate of secondary importance, he did not hold any key positions in Congress or play a primary role in formulating policy.[1]

On July 11, 1776, the day it received the first official news of independence, the Council of Safety resolved to replace the ailing Oliver Wolcott, who had returned to Connecticut. The Council felt that Connecticut should be fully represented at such a critical juncture and decided to send Williams. He left for Philadelphia on July 22 and arrived on the twenty-eighth. The trip was the "most tiresome, sultry, and fatigueing" he had ever made, a journey rendered even more unpleasant by "a severe Touch of the quick Step (according to Army Phrase)" upon his arrival. Almost immediately he began expressing the wish to go home. The weather in Philadelphia was the hottest he had ever experienced, and he missed his family. He left the city on November 12, one month after Oliver Wolcott's return. Wolcott believed that Williams returned to Connecticut at this time because "he did not know of any particular personal or Family Intrest to induce him to tarry longer." Williams did actively promote the interests of his Trumbull-in-laws, so Wolcott's statement is truthful. But he desired for personal reasons to leave Congress and he departed as soon as possible. He attended Congress again in 1777. This time, Williams, Dyer, and Richard Law took their seats on June 25. Williams continued to serve until December 2, 1777, when he and Law obtained leaves of absence. Williams was chosen to attend Congress in October, 1783, and May, 1784, but failed to attend.[2]

The political views of delegate Williams were not unusual. He forwarded the interests of his friends and relatives, and he represented the interests of Connecticut and the New England bloc. More out of the ordinary was his extreme religiosity and intense parochialism. Williams' Puritan conception of the trials the nation was enduring is exemplified by a letter he wrote to the Governor on September 20, 1776, just after the evacuation of New York. The victories gained by the enemy and the distresses of the country all gave "loudspeaking testimonies of the displeasure and Anger of Almighty God against a sinful people." God must assuredly be angry at the American people and will either bring them to repentance and reformation or destroy them. Americans had always believed that God was with them, but they had not repented. "It is God who has blunted the weapons of our warfare . . . that has, thus far, blasted and disappointed our hopes, and made us flee before our enemies." Williams had always thought that America's cause was just and rightous and that God would vindicate and support it. He still believed so.

> But I believe this people must first be brought to know and acknowledge the rightousness of his judgements, and their own exceeding sinfulness and guilt, and be deeply humbled under his mighty hand, and look, and cry to, and trust in Him, for all their help and salvation. . . . Why are not the dear children of God . . . besieging the Throne of Grace, sighing and crying for their own sins and backslidings, and for all the abominations that we are done in the land, saying, "Spare, spare thy people, O Lord![3]

Like so many other Americans, Williams was extremely narrow-minded and parochial. He disliked the French, New Yorkers, southerners, indeed, almost everyone who did not live in New England. He opposed French aid. Americans should depend on the justice of the cause and the infinite mercy of God, not "the Help of Foreigners." The next year, due to the promises of Commissioner Silas Deane in Paris, Philadelphia was overrun with unemployed French officers expecting high military appointments. Williams scornfully commented, "I forbear to say many things, the City swarms with French men."[4] His dislike of the City of Brotherly Love is, perhaps, understandable. Prices were outrageous, the population lukewarm towards the American cause, the weather was stiffling, and the city spawned disease. When he first arrived in 1776, he contracted a severe case of diarrhea and after his arrival in 1777, he fell victim to a "Rhematic Pain" which affected his right arm and wrist. The disease incapacitated him for a month and a half. Not until August 19 could he again attend the meetings of Congress in the city which Williams considered "the mother of Harlots."[5] Referring to Pennsylvanians generally, he asserted that they had "a fixed hatred of N. E. and every thing that belongs to it, but Money, and that is all the God they worship." Williams' attitude towards southerners was no more enlightened. "There seems to be Spirit in some of the South agst. the no[r]thern Colonies and all their Officers and Affairs." Yorkers enjoyed the special disdain of New Englanders. The New England delegates attempted in 1776 and 1777 to dismiss General Schuyler from command of the northern army, an effort that caused "great heart burning in many members," who will "curse N[ew] Engl[an]d." When Schuyler was finally replaced by Virginian Horatio Gates in August, 1777, the move was strenuously opposed by all delegates from New York and unanimously supported by New Englanders. Williams hoped that "N England will take their own measures to drive Burgoyne into the Lakes, without waiting for Congress." In general, Williams believed that most delegates hated New England and persecuted every New England man.[6]

Williams and the other Connecticut delegates became deeply embroiled in personal controversies, the most difficult and exasperating concerning the ambitions and hypersensitivity of the sons of Governor Trumbull. Williams, the Governor's son-in-law, naturally devoted much attention to the affairs of Joseph, Jonathan, Jr., and John Trumbull. He tried to protect their political flanks in Philadelphia and secure favorable appointments for them. He endeavored to win a raise for Joseph, the Commissary General; he tried to satisfy the complaints of Jonathan, Jr., Paymaster General for the Northern Department; and he succeeded in securing the post of Deputy Adjutant General for twenty-one year old John Trumbull, the budding painter. Joseph resigned in July, 1777, and the Connecticut delegates urged in vain that he accept a position on the War Board. He refused, in part, because Williams, perhaps from credulity or exasperation, repeated rumors based on the authority of an anonymous informer that Congress doubted Joseph's integrity. Trumbull, the report stated, aimed to frustrate the activities of the Commissary Department because of anger over Congress' treatment of him. The Trumbulls were incensed at the charge, but Eliphalet Dyer advised Joseph to pay no attention.

> I should have thot the Govr and you had been long enough acquainted with Coll. Williams. I mean the suddeness of his Temper, the warmth of his Imagination, the strong Impression sometimes a little matter makes on his mind (tho' of an honest good heart) to lay so great a Stress upon his painting. I found he had wrote and feard as for some other of his letters. They were unguarded and would have no good effect, but the Contrary.[7]

The episode left a sour taste in the mouths of all participants.

Although it may be only coincidence, the next year, for the first time, Williams publicly disagreed with the Governor, over price regulation. Williams also endeavored to aid the careers of political allies in Connecticut. He secured a major's commission for Eliphalet Dyer's son, and he evidenced sectional anger at the dismissal of General Wooster, an action prompted by military failures in Canada.[8]

He had the satisfaction just before his departure from Congress to see the recall of his old enemy Silas Deane. Deane had powerful foes in Congress and his native state, among them the Lees, the Adams, Roger Sherman, Eliphalet Dyer, and William Williams. Hostility to Deane had arisen as a mob of Frenchmen descended on Philadelphia in 1777, all brandishing commissions granted by Deane. The motion to remove him was introduced in July, but it was not acted upon until November 21. The motion was "carried without a dissenting Voice. He [Deane] died at last very easie, tho there had been at sund[ry] Times before, the most violent and convulsive throes and Exertions on the same Question."[9]

Congressman Williams served primarily on lesser committees. On August 27, 1776, he was one of four persons added to a committee to revise the journals of the Congress and to superintend their printing. Congress delegated Williams and one representative from each other state on September 25 to employ persons to purchase blankets and woolens for soldiers' clothing. On October 1, he was one of a committee of five chosen to prepare a plan for a military academy. Only towards the end of his congressional career was he appointed to a major committee. Congress added Williams and three others to the Board of War on October 17, 1777.[10]

During the summer of 1776, Congress wrestled with an attempt to draft the "Articles of Confederation and Perpetual Union." Beginning July 22, Congress debated the "Articles" in committee of the whole for twenty days. Progress ground to a halt in deep disagreements over representation, taxation, and western lands. Williams accurately expressed the situation on August 7. "We make slow Progress [he wrote] . . . as every Inch of Ground is disputed . . . I almost Despair of seeing it accomplished." As argument followed argument and debate after debate brought no decision, Congress reached a deadlock. Williams wrote that although everyone seemed "to labour hard," he feared "a permanent one will never be settled," especially after the Maryland delegates walked out. "What will be the event of Things, God only knows." Soon afterwards, the Articles were dropped from consideration, because antagonisms were too deep to be reconciled. Tempers could be cooled and progress on other matters forwarded by dropping the plan of confederation.[11]

Admiral Lord Howe arrived in America in mid-July, commanding the British fleet and heading a peace commission. He had the authority to reconcile Britain and America, but his powers were limited to granting pardons. Once Congress learned that his powers were so meager, it showed little interest in his proposals. But after Washington had been humiliated in the battle of Long Island, Lord Howe believed that Congress would be more receptive. He sent captured General John Sullivan to Philadelphia with a new olive branch that appeared more substantial then this earlier one. Sullivan delivered Howe's message on September 2, and Congress debated the matter for four days. Although few, if any, had any hope for peace, they finally ordered "three Members, in their proper Character only, to wait on Ld Howe . . . to know if He has power to treat of Peace, what his Power is, and to hear his Propositions." Howe wished to speak with the delegation as private men, but Congress would only send them "as a Deputation of their Body." Williams clearly articulated the feelings of Congress when he stated that if the Admiral did not receive them in their capacity as delegates, "the World will be satisfied there is no sincerity in his Professions." The three delegates, Franklin, John Adams, and Edward Rutledge, returned on September 13. Howe informed the committee that he had no power to treat with them as members of Congress, and that no terms could be proposed "without a full return to their Allegiance." They had expected no more, but Williams believed that one important point had been gained. The affair would "strike the Torys dumb." It would "defeat and kill the impression they were makeing . . . on many Friendly but credulous Minds by their confident . . . Assertions, that Ld H. was vested with full and ample Powers to settle the Controversie on the most equitable Terms."[12]

Congress concerned itself in the fall of 1776 with drawing up plans to secure foreign alliances. It adopted a plan for a treaty with France, appointed agents to execute the task, and adopted instructions to guide them. Colonel Williams evidenced little interest in these affairs and devoted himself to exchanging war news with his friends in Connecticut and advancing their interests.[13]

Congress tackled five major problems during Williams' tenure in 1777 — Howe's invasion of Pennsylvania, the northern campaign, the influx of French officers, currency depreciation, and the Articles of Confederation. Until August 19, Williams was too ill to attend the meetings of Congress, although he maintained a desultory correspondence with his friends in Connecticut and did reluctantly attend a celebration of American independence. "Yesterday was in my opinion poorly spent in celebrating the anniversary of ye Declaration of Independence." He only attended the public entertainments "to avoid Singularity & Reflection upon my dear Colony." He noted with disdain that "a great Expenditure of Liquor, Powder &c took up ye Day, & of Candles thro ye City [a] good part of the night, I suppose & conclude much Tory unilluminated Glass will want replacing."[14]

General Howe decided, instead of marching up the Hudson to join Burgoyne, to attack Philadelphia. But rather than take the risks of an overland march, however, he embarked with his army and sailed up Chesapeake Bay, landing at Head of Elk on August 25. By that evening, Congress had learned the alarming news and the Connecticut delegates reported to Governor Trumbull, "Philadelphia may yet be his principal object." Williams, however, was not totally depressed at the turn of events. "Indeed, were it not for the abounding sins & wholly unreformed state of the country, I sho'd dare hope that God in mercy had blinded the minds & darkned the councils of enemies & turned them into foolishness." Although he did not know what the future would bring, he accurately observed that the British "had lost the season." They could not hope to achieve victory in 1777. Howe's forces had lived at sea for six weeks. This event had rendered "their troops sickly" and, more importantly, Howe could not "join & cooperate with Burgoyne, or fall upon other parts of N. England." It was "certain N. England has vast occasion to bless & praise the Lord for his wondrous mercy in our deliverance from the dreadful scourge." The situation in the north looked promising. The northern army was now commanded by officers trusted by New England, and recent military events — the relief of Fort Stanwix and General Stark's victory at Bennington — offered the hope of ultimate success. If the people of New England exerted themselves, "they may by the blessing of Heaven effect a most happy close to the present warr before this year expires."[15]

On September 11, however, Washington's army suffered defeat in the battle of Brandywine and this convinced Williams that the citizens of Philadelphia had little enthusiasm for the war. "The people of ye city seem to be little stirred, & but very little. They are amazingly stupid and seem to think no harm will come to them. . . . Indeed tis hard for me to say whether ye greater part will not be well pleased with Howe's success." Recent events had revealed the displeasure of God and represented "a sure sign that more dreadful evils await us." Congress voted to remove from Philadelphia. It left on September 18, and eight days later Howe's army entered the city. Though the disasters in Pennsylvania were extremely dismaying, the morale of Congress rose with news from the north. On September 30, Williams reported that letters had come from General Gates and the news served to "exhillerate the Spirits of Congress." Congress received unofficial news of Burgoyne's surrender on October 26, and this report lifted Williams's spirits. "What infinite reason have We to bless & extol ye name of ye Lord of Hosts, ye God of Armys."[16]

Congress again took up the Articles of Confederation in April, 1777, but, by the time Williams had returned, "very little progress . . . in ye Confederation" had been made. Further debates occurred throughout the summer, but it was not until after their exile to Yorktown that the delegates firmly agreed that they must confederate or perish. The most crucial question involved representation, whether voting should be by state or by population. The final vote took place on October 14, 1777. Two proposals for proportional representation were overwhelmingly defeated, and the delegates voted, with only Virginia opposing, that each state would have one vote. Connecticut was a small state, and the delegation unanimously supported voting by state. Next in importance was the apportionment of taxes. Connecticut and the other New England states wanted financial contributions to the central government to be proportional to population. But Congress decided, five states to four, with two divided, to apportion expenses on the basis of land values with their improvements. Connecticut never reconciled itself to this mode of taxation, and the delegation repeatedly endeavored in vain to reverse Congress' decision. The third question involved control of western lands. The state was overpopulated and the soil poor, thus to Connecticut the acquisition of additional territory was of vital importance. Congress resolved on October 15, with only Maryland dissenting, that it had no control over territories claimed by the several states. Once these questions were decided, work on the Articles proceeded smoothly. On November 15, the Articles of Confederation were completed and recorded in the journals of Congress. Two days later they were sent to the states for their approbation.[17] Except for the provision on taxation, Williams was satisfied with the document, and upon his return to Connecticut he worked for its approval.

The state acted quickly on the Articles. Governor Trumbull ordered three hundred copies printed and distributed to the towns. Over half the towns convened in late December and January to discuss the new constitution, and Lebanon was among forty-five communities that explicitly approved them. The inhabitants of Lebanon assembled on January 1, 1778, and they agreed that a plan of union for common defense, security for their liberties and general welfare, and for assisting one another against their enemies was necessary in order to maintain the freedom, liberty, and independence of the states. The Articles of Confederation were "in substance well and wisely calculated to answer ye great & important purposes for which they are designed." Article Eight, however, which specified that common expenses were to be divided proportionally among the states according to the value of all lands, they did not consider the best or most "practicable rule & criterion of assessing ye proportion of each State." They urged the General Assembly to get Article Eight changed, but if that was impossible, the article together with all the rest should be ratified. Many other towns objected to the eighth article and the Lower House, "after large dispute," passed it only "by a small majority." The Lower House approved the plan in January, but the Council delayed giving its approval until February.[18]

Congress and Connecticut labored without notable success to halt the rapid depreciation of continental currency and the equally sharp escalation of wages and prices. Emission after emission poured forth from state and continental presses, while war costs and taxes shot upwards. Williams, like Puritan statesman Roger Sherman, firmly supported currency regulation and price controls. He favored both limitations on currency emission and additional state taxation to meet federal expenses, and he was alarmed by the exorbitant rise in prices and the depreciation of currency. Congress possessed "no practicable way to remedy the great and growing [evil] but a firm Union to establish the Credit of the [currency] which the Tribe of Speculators . . . begin to pick Flaws in," a firm resolve to limit the quantity of bills in circulation, and a determination to meet "future expenses by Taxation."[19]

The Connecticut Assembly valiantly attempted to fight inflation and to bear the burdens of war through increased taxation and price controls. State taxes increased dramatically from a prewar average of one or two pence on the pound to a rate of two shillings and eleven pence by the close of 1777. Connecticut also resorted to the printing press, issuing £1,200,000 in paper currency. Price controls began in November, 1776, and, although new statutes were continually being enacted, prices climbed steadily. The townspeople of Lebanon expressed Williams' convictions, when on March 31, 1777, they declared that laws to prevent excessive prices were "founded in principals of Humanity, Justice, & Policy."[20]

By early 1778, Governor Trumbull, responding to the interests of Connecticut merchants, argued that price controls were useless, but he could not prevent passage in February, 1778, of a final rigorous act to regulate the prices of labor, produce, and manufactures. Williams favored the act, and thus, for the first time, broke with the Trumbulls. The decision was a difficult one. "It was with much consideration [he wrote to Jonathan Trumbull, Jr.] that I settled my opinion in favr of ye regulating Act & with great reluctance, peculiarly on Acco[unt] of its not agreeing with ye judgm[en]t of yr Father." He seriously considered not voting until "strenuously checked by some of ye Board." It was no crime to vote according to the dictates of one's conscience, he added. During the same special session, a report spread that at least one of the Governor's sons had acquired an excessively large quantity of rum. Evidently Williams believed the rumor and helped spread it. He asserted defensively that he believed the story true, and that if that was "a Crime, I am guilty."[21] Either consciously or unconsciously, Williams, by these actions, began to separate himself from the Trumbulls and was expressing his disenchantment with their mercantile bias. Congress, too, had become convinced by 1778 that price regulations did not work and recommended that all such legistation be repealed. Connecticut followed Congress' recommendation. Ironically, although wide popular support for price controls still existed, the refusal of Connecticut farmers to sell beef at regulated prices forced Congress to ask for the suspension of these laws.[22]

The continued rapid increase in prices and the downward spiral of the value of continental currency led to new efforts to re-impose price controls. The sentiment in favor of regulation waxed strongest in Windham County. On June 1, 1779, the inhabitants of Windham voted to appoint a committee to communicate with other towns in the county to see what measures could be taken to halt further price increases. Lebanon responded affirmatively on September 3 by appointing William Williams, Vetch Williams, and four others a committee to meet with other towns to consider proper and constitutional means to check further price increases and further currency depreciation. The Windham County Convention, meeting on September 6, endorsed all efforts to stop additional depreciation and urged that a state convention be held in Hartford in October. The convention designated William Williams, Nathaniel Wales, Jr., and Hezekiah Bissel a committee of correspondence. The inhabitants of Lebanon convened again on September 14, endorsed the recommendations of the convention, and appointed Williams and Joshua West to attend the convention in Hartford. A majority of towns, however, by now opposed new price controls that the delegates recommended, and inflation hurtled completely out of control. Recognizing the inevitable, Congress in March, 1780, devalued its currency to one-fortieth of its original value and the Connnecticut legislature followed suit. Devaluation destroyed what little public confidence remained, and the downward spiral continued.[23]

The Governor's opposition to price controls cost him popular support, particularly in control-conscious Windham County. Rumors began to circulate in the spring of 1780 of Trumbull making a fortune from illicit trade with the enemy. These stories began in Windham and Mansfield, two strongholds of price regulation. Williams reported to the Governor that rumors were circulating there that he had "lately sent two Vessells with Grain to Long Island." Because of these reports, Trumbull failed to receive a majority of the votes cast, and Williams lost his Council seat. The decline in the Governor's popularity resulted from dissatisfaction by the supporters of price controls, war weariness, and unhappiness with Trumbull's leadership. William Williams found himself caught in the fallout. On the one hand, he lost votes because he was too closely identified with Governor Trumbull and thus with his economic policies, and, on the other hand, he lost support because the merchant party opposed him because of his approval of price controls. Williams was so closely identified with a vigorous war effort that he found himself caught in a war-fatigue backlash. Moreverover, his strict Calvinism and personal rivalries with the merchant friends of Silas Deane also earned him enmity. The animosity to Williams was so great that, although a vacancy on the Council occurred with the resignation of Jabez Huntington and the Upper House wanted to reappoint Williams, the Lower House refused.[24]

He had not, however, lost the respect of his townsmen, for they elected him to the Lower House in September, 1780. The resentment towards him in that body was temporary. The Assembly still held Williams in high esteem, but the House did not believe that he should be elevated to the Council, except by popular will. The Lower House immediately elected him Clerk, and in May, 1781, chose him Speaker, a position he held until he was returned to the Council in May, 1784. But the Assembly, nevertheless, chose Williams, Dyer, and Andrew Adams a committee to meet with commissioners from other New England states at Hartford in November, 1780. The commissioners were directed to determine the proper means for filling quotas in the Continental Army and supplying them. Shortly thereafter, Williams, Adams, and Jeremiah Wadsworth were appointed to meet with commissioners from other states in Providence "to consider what may be proper and necessary . . . to place the purchase of provisions for the fleet and army of his Most Christian Majesty, and for the army of the United States, upon a footing mutually advantageous to both." They were also empowered on behalf of the state to enter into a supply contract with agents appointed by the French.[25]

In addition to his duties in Congress, the legislature, and the Council of Safety, Williams held the office of Selectman of Lebanon. The Selectmen had always been the plural chief executive and the administrative officials in the towns. War, of course, had magnified their duties. The towns dealt with all kinds of wartime problems ranging from the confining of Tories and combatting inflation to raising, feeding, and clothing troops.[26] The activities of the community in providing supplies for the families of indigent soldiers, collecting clothing and provisions for Lebanon's soldiers in the Continental Army, and securing recruits to fill the town's quota were of particular importance. The Council of Safety believed that some persons may have been discouraged from enlisting because they lacked the resources to care for their families in their absence. In order to lessen this concern, the Council, in March, 1777, directed every town to take care of its families of poor soldiers. The towns were to appoint committees to provide food at fixed prices to the families, on condition that the soldiers would in the future repay the money advanced by the local committee. The Lebanon Selectmen called a town meeting for March 3, 1777, and the inhabitants voted to do everything in their power to encourage enlistments. They chose a committee to provide necessities to the families of indigent soldiers on the request of the soldier or his family. New committees to provide the same service were chosen by the town each year until 1781. The aid was not conceived as charity, for it was always intended that the soldiers would reimburse the town for the money expended, but it is unlikely that compensation was often made, and the care of these families just added to the town's welfare load.[27]

The Council of Safety in September, 1777, ordered each town to properly clothe its own soldiers. On September 24, the town of Lebanon appointed a committee to purchase the articles of clothing needed. Each non-commissioned officer and enlisted man was to be provided with one hunting shirt, one linen or flannel shirt, one pair of overalls, one pair of shoes, and two pairs of socks. In the later stages of the war, the town also incurred the responsibility for raising provisions for the Continental Army. The General Assembly, in October, 1779, in compliance with an urgent plea from General Washington, directed each town to provide flour and grain for the troops. Lebanon's quota was figured at 116 bushels of wheat and 150 bushels of rye. In 1780 and 1781, the town levied three special taxes to purchase Lebanon's quota of grain and flour.[28]

War weariness had set in by the spring of 1777, and thereafter the town was hard-pressed to raise its quota of recruits for continental service. The town endeavored valiantly, but with only partial success, to encourage enlistments, and the inhabitants taxed themselves heavily to provide bounties. On one occasion, in the summer of 1780, when Lebanon was short forty-seven recruits, the town granted a bounty of £6 in silver or grain annually for persons enlisting for three years, and forty shillings a month for wages. A tax of three pence on the pound in gold, silver, or grain was levied for that purpose. Military service, except perhaps for the officer corps, was a singularly unattractive occupation, and inflation, economic dislocations, and wartime shortages made it even more so. Despite the efforts of Williams and others, it is questionable if, after 1778, the town's quota was ever filled.[29]

In July, 1780, six regiments of French troops, commanded by the

Comte de Rochambeau, landed and established headquarters near Newport, Rhode Island. The costs of horses, foodstuffs, and grain climbed so rapidly that Rochambeau was obliged to search for special quarters for his cavalry unit, the Legion of Hussars commanded by the Duke de Lauzun. In October, the Assembly, on Rochambeau's application, directed that quarters be provided for Lauzun's cavalry in eastern Connecticut. Some two hundred and twenty hussars were stationed in Lebanon·from the end of November, 1780, to June 23, 1781. The Williams family enjoyed the dubious distinction of quartering Colonel Dillon, one of the unit's officers. Williams, who was attending meetings of the legislature in New Haven, first heard the news at the end of October, and he composed an agitated letter to his wife. "I hear a half Story that You are taking in some French Gentry. I dont know what to make of it. I wish you had wrote to me something about it." Colonel Williams still had not given his approval as late as November 18, when Jonathan Trumbull, Jr., wrote that "Mrs. Williams is concerned about taking Mons[ieu]r Dillon" and she wanted her husband's advice on the subject. Williams' duty was clear, however, and on November 23, the Colonel's servants arrived with his baggage, while Dillon appeared the next day.[30]

Relations between the French officers and the Williams were "correct," but Colonel and Mrs. Williams were displeased by French extravagance, vanity, and conceit. On February 26, 1781, the Duke de Lauzun informed Williams that the French man of war *L'Eveille*, a sixty-four, had captured the British man of war *Romulus*, fifty guns, together with eight transports and five hundred men. In mid-March, the Duke accepted an invitation to breakfast at the Williams home. The behavior of the French troops was generally good, but since they were unpaid, far removed from the actual fighting, their commanding officer often absent, and their foodstuffs often less than choice, by late winter, discipline had slackened. Writing on behalf of his brother, Dr. Thomas Williams, the Colonel complained to the Duke that the conduct of the French was much worse than they had expected. From Dr. Williams, they had stolen wood, fence, four or five sheep, geese, and many other articles and had, moveover, cut down more than thirty trees. Williams recognized that it was difficult to punish individuals without proof, and the difficulties were compounded by the language problem. But he hoped the Duke would be able to halt the depredations, and then the French would regain their good impression. The French finally departed on June 23, an event that occurred none too soon for Mary Williams.

> O how glad & how thankfull I shall be when Theay are gone, [she wrote] for never was I so sick of any people in my Life. . . . [I] wish never to see another French man in my live, the best of them are notheing but pride & vanity.[31]

The Legion took part in the crucial Yorktown campaign, and it was primarily due to French military and naval support that Lord Cornwallis was forced on October 17, 1781, to surrender.

Six weeks before Yorktown, the British launched their most vicious blow upon Connecticut, when forces commanded by Benedict Arnold, in an effort to relieve pressure on Cornwallis, burned New London and overwhelmed the defenders of Fort Griswold in Groton. Williams heard the news the same day and, according to tradition, rode twenty-three miles in three hours to New London in order to fight the enemy. But the veracity of the story is questionable. Two extant letters dated September 6 at six o'clock in the evening and September 7 at seven in the morning and posted from Lebanon, give no evidence of any such journey. Williams reported news of the attack to Governor Trumbull as received by an express rider, but no hint is given that he had been at the scene of the tragedy.[32] The peace treaty was not signed for another two years, troops continued to be raised, and the Council of Safety continued to deliberate, but in essence the war ended at Yorktown in October, 1781.

Williams engaged actively in all aspects of the war effort in Connecticut. He served conscientiously, although without distinction, in Congress, and he ardently promoted the fight for independence from the Upper House, the Council of Safety, and from the position of Selectman of Lebanon. He worked constantly to animate the war effort. His own sacrifices were substantial, while the exertions of his home town were also of consequence. It was due to the efforts of patriots like Williams that Connecticut's efforts in behalf of independence were so generous. Williams' single-minded devotion to the cause cost him needed popular support, while his devotion to price controls and his religious interpretation of the trials the nation was enduring, is evidence that he hoped victory would bring a new dawn of virtue and piety to America. God had punished Connecticut and America for their sins, but salvation could be hoped for through prayer, faith in God, repentance, devotion to duty, honesty, and virtue. These traits Williams carried with him throughout the years of struggle. He did not profit monetarily or politically from the war; indeed, the reverse proved true. Although the new world of the 1780s contained many elements of which an old-fashioned Whig could not approve, still he could look back with satisfaction on the role he had played in driving Connecticut towards independence and in fighting to preserve it.

The Final Years

WILLIAM WILLIAMS lived for thirty years after the battle of York-town and was politically active for more than twenty of them. The main responsibility for the emergence of factionalism in Connecticut in the 1780s belonged to Congress, and the split between nationalists and agrarians provided the vehicle by which Williams regained his Council seat in 1784. In 1780, when the war was at its lowest ebb, Congress promised half pay for life to all continental officers who agreed to serve for the duration. Such special privileges for a small elite aroused great hostility in Congress, so in 1782, half pay for life was commuted to full pay for five years and three months back pay. Half pay stirred intense opposition among the townspeople of Lebanon and many others in the state, and commutation earned even more hatred. Unprecedented wartime taxation, inflation, economic difficulties, and resentment of the Trumbulls occasioned this hostility to special privileges for the officer corps. Governor Trumbull and the merchant nationalists supported half pay, while Williams, Puritan, agrarian, provincial, and contemptuous of the greedy profiteer, opposed. He separated himself from the Trumbulls, allied himself with majoritarian sentiment in Lebanon and Connecticut, and, in consequence, won back his Council seat. The people of Lebanon in April, 1782, instructed their representatives, William Williams and Captain Daniel Tilden, to oppose half pay. Williams penned the instructions. The expenses of war had imposed heavy burdens upon all, and it was of vital importance that economy be the rule for all public expenditures. "All who serve ye Public shod eat ye public Bread . . . but none ought to eat ye Bread of Idleness . . . especially [in] a War undertaken for necessary Defense of Liberty & property agnst Oppression." Williams condemned half pay as "unconstitutional, injurious, impolitic, oppressive, & unjust" and tending to promote idleness, excess, extravagance, and corruption. Lebanon's deputies were enjoined to do everything in their power to prevent such an establishment.[1] The exertions of war had not, in Williams' eyes, noticeably improved man's character. In promoting the glorious cause, it had to be expected that many unnecessary burdens and evil expenses would occur due to "the Weakness and Wickedness of Mankind." It did not follow, however, that frauds, corruptions, and extravagance in the form of impolitic grants and stipends "ought to be patiently borne, but by all lawful means to be guarded against & avoided."[2] The Assembly appointed a committee to examine pension grants in May, but it took no further action.

News of commutation reached Connecticut in early 1783, and it served to lessen the popularity of the nationalist governor. Trumbull earned barely one-third of the votes, and he agreed reluctantly to serve another year only after being overwhelmingly endorsed by the Assembly. The freemen of Lebanon on April 28, 1783, roundly condemned commutation and instructed their representatives to exert themselves in every lawful way to oppose pay for officers, which they considered a violation of Article Eight of the Articles of Confederation, and to support the freedom and sovereignty of the states against all attempts to subjugate them. The Lower House, with Williams in the Speaker's chair, approved a remonstrance to Congress, but the more nationally-minded Council refused to concur. The commutation issue boiled over into a full-fledged political debate between nationalists and anti-commutationists over the powers of Congress and the necessity of supporting it.[3]

Lebanon split politically for the first time in history. The nationalists, led by the Trumbulls, remained a minority until after the adoption of the Constitution. Williams seized the leadership of the anti-nationalists, and his example was followed by most of the other political leaders in town. Burdened by taxes and inflation, the people of Lebanon lashed out against commutation, which, they believed, would increase their taxes in order to benefit the few, a minority whose sacrifices had been no greater than their own. When the Trumbulls took the nationalist side, they opposed the wishes of their constituents and paid the political consequences.

Two extra-legal conventions were held in Middletown in September, 1783, at which Lebanon was represented. The Convention aimed at devising constitutional measures to oppose commutation and changing the makeup of the nationalist Council. The legislature, in October, approved a remonstrance to Congress, but the conventioners gained greater success. The terms of the pro-commutation Congressmen had expired, and three of the four new delegates sympathized with the Convention — James Wadsworth, William Hillhouse, and William Williams. In addition, "the Convultion of the People & ye Middletown Convention has produced a Shift in the Nomination, tho not greater than was expected." Two of the most senior Councillors, Eliphalet Dyer, a member of the Upper House since 1762, and Abraham Davenport, a member since 1766, were left off the nominations list, and five new men appeared. Deputy Governor Griswold was also excluded, and, in the *greatest* coup, the Governor, too, was left out. Williams sorrowfully told his wife that "Your Father has laid in his Resignation to the very great Grief of ye most valuable & a numerous part of ye Assembly & People." The October, 1783, session of the legislature marked the high tide for the Middletown Convention, and by the time of the spring elections, the force had gone out of the movement. Only one of the seven persons the Convention had proposed for the Council was elected, Williams, who recaptured his Council seat, not primarily due to his political views, but because of the peculiarities of Connecticut's electoral system. Three vacancies existed on the Council. Davenport and Dyer had not been re-nominated, and Samuel Huntington was elevated to lieutenant governor. Williams, a former Assistant, ranked eleventh on the nominations list, ahead of all other non-incumbents, and, under normal circumstances, the first fourteen on the list, Governor, Lieutenant Governor, and twelve Assistants, gained election.[4] Williams won back his seat on the Council because of his seniority and ranking on the nominations list, not because he was known as an opponent of commutation.[5] As a former Assistant and present Speaker, it would have been unrealistic to expect that he would not win.

Williams regretted deeply the fate of his father-in-law and, unlike many other anti-commutationists, was not a doctrinaire supporter of state sovereignty. He favored, for example, the continental impost, which the Lower House rejected in October, 1783.[6] Personal conviction and an awareness of political advantage combined to thrust him into the forefront of the anti-nationalist cause between 1783 and 1787, and he was probably the best-known and most powerful political figure in that faction.

Although commutation burned out as an issue, new tensions arose over the Society of the Cincinnati, the Western Reserve, and the emission of paper money. Some localists were motivated by political ambition, others by the interests of state creditors, others by resentment against profiteering merchants, and interior farmers by heavy taxation. Nationalists, led by Trumbull and a majority on the Council, represented established political leadership concerned with preserving the *status quo*. They wanted to see the authority of Congress respected, and they were supported by continental security holders, merchants, and officers in the Continental Army. The Society of the Cincinnati was organized to further the interests of the officer corps of the army. The Cincinnati members in Connecticut elected Samuel Holden Parsons and Jonathan Trumbull, Jr., President and Secretary of the local chapter. Cincinnati, nationalists, and continental creditors wanted to sell lands in Connecticut's Western Reserve, sight-unseen, in five-thousand-acre tracts. The land was to be paid for in either specie, Continental securities, or state securities. Localists and state creditors, who controlled the Lower House, wanted to use the Western Reserve for the benefit of the people and as a means of paying off the state debt. They proposed that the area be surveyed before settlement, be divided into townships, and payment in Continental securities be prohibited.

Williams distrusted the Cincinnati, believing it hostile to democracy, and he opposed their western land program. A letter he wrote on the subject was stolen and printed in the *Connecticut Courant* on October 9, 1784, together with a burlesque version signed by "William Wimble," a name that became identified with him and was used in other forgeries. The Connecticut Wits, who ridiculed Williams, were nationalists, and the overly sensitive and proud Councillor responded by accusing General Parsons of hiring the Wits to deride him. Although Parsons denied the charge, nationalists worked fruitlessly to unseat him. Their ridicule increased in December, 1786, when Judge Williams adjourned the Windham County Court. Nationalists accused Williams of being under the influence of the Shaysites. The charge was absurd. He dismissed the Court because of inclement weather and the scarcity of money. Williams believed that the people were exerting themselves to the utmost, and would probably settle many debts before the next court. He added as an afterthought to his denial of the charge "that the pressure of debts on the people of Massachusetts . . . had a principal hand in exciting the tumults and confusions in that state." He then adjourned the Court to the usual time in February.[7]

These machinations did Williams no harm, for in May, 1787, he received 3,532 votes, third highest in the state, and he also polled 958 votes for Lieutenant Governor, a post won by Oliver Wolcott. Williams knew of the efforts being made on his behalf and claimed he had nothing to do with them. "You well know," he told his wife, "I did not wish it & had determined to refuse, but am relieved I had 900 & odd Votes & Mr Wolcott had 2200."[8]

The climax of the struggle between nationalists and localists occurred with Connecticut's adoption of the new federal Constitution. In October, 1787, the legislature voted unanimously to call a special convention for January 4, 1788, to consider the document. William Williams and Ephraim Carpenter were selected by Lebanon town meeting to attend the convention. Jonathan Trumbull, Jr., was disqualified because of his nationalist views. The Lebanon townspeople, after considerable rancor, resolved to instruct their delegates to oppose the Constitution. Captain Carpenter obeyed his instructions and cast one of the forty votes against the Constitution, but Williams violated them and voted in favor. He objected to one clause in the document, the one which provided that no religious test shall ever be required for any public office. Although he thought all religious tests were useless, he still believed that the document ought to include a formal statement of religious principle. Despite the fact that he had been elected as an anti-Federalist, he was not a confirmed foe of government. Although philosophically an Old Whig and an advocate of state sovereignty, he realized that Connecticut's identity could only be preserved by radical changes in the federal system. He could see that ratification was certain, and he followed the path of political wisdom by voting with the majority. Williams could also have been influenced by events in Lebanon.

After serving as Selectman for twenty-seven years, he, along with all other incumbents, was abruptly dropped in December, 1786. He resented this treatment and was alarmed by the men who deposed him. They wanted to recreate old committees of correspondence on grievances, "demolish Lawyers, enlarge ye power of Justices, & create a new mode of administering Justice." It tortured him "to Madness to see a happy people rush headlong, wilfully blind, to destruction."[9] Williams saw the specter of Shaysism in the actions of his townsmen, and this may have influenced him to vote for ratification. Perhaps, too, feeling betrayed by his constituents, he no longer felt morally obligated to obey instructions whose wisdom he doubted. Williams' political judgement was correct, for Federalism became dominant in the state and in Lebanon. Jonathan Trumbull, the younger, who previously was considered too nationalistic to be elected to the Assembly, earned forgiveness from the town, was elected to the legislature in May, 1788, and was immediately chosen Speaker. Lebanon's rebellion against the Trumbull's leadership, motivated by economic difficulties and led by William Williams, ended.

*

Williams remained politically active throughout the 1790s. He became the senior Assistant in 1789 and thus headed the nominations list. He continued to serve as Judge of Probate and Judge of the County Court. He corresponded with old associates like Samuel Adams, Josiah Bartlett, Roger Sherman, and Jonathan Trumbull, Jr., and became a loyal member of the Federalist Party. Through exchanges with Trumbull, he kept abreast of national affairs and was responsible for writing a petition from the town of Lebanon in support of the Jay Treaty. Since he was the senior member of the Council, he was returned to office every May, but he was by no means the most popular Assistant. Until the mid-1790s, his vote total placed him in the middle of that for incumbent Councillors. In May, 1792, for example, he polled 3,128 votes, ranking him sixth in popularity, and in October, 1793, he had the seventh highest number of votes among the nominees. But in October, 1794, as a result of the blocking by the Council of an act to repeal the western lands appropriation act, he placed twentieth and last on the nominations list, polling just twenty-seven votes more than Gideon Granger, Jr. Williams was not the only incumbent to fare poorly. Only one of the six senior Assistants stood in the top ten in votes, and Lieutenant Governor Oliver Wolcott wound up thirtieth and failed to be listed among the nominees. Popular wrath subsided the following year and Williams was re-elected, which he could scarcely fail to be because he was listed first, and in October, 1795, he ranked seventh in votes. Thereafter Williams' popularity declined and his vote ranked among the lowest for successful officeholders. As a representative of an earlier era, his political ideas and his stern religion alienated the more cosmopolitan voters. His staunch Federalism, too, may have cost him votes. Most significant, however, was widespread dislike of the electoral system. The ranking of incumbent Councillors by seniority instead of popularity made it extremely difficult for incumbents to be displaced, and since William Williams was listed first, angry voters could take out their resentments against the system by cutting the senior Assistant.[10]

In October, 1801, Williams polled the third highest total of votes, because he headed a preliminary nominations list prepared by Jeffersonians. He had nothing to do with these plans, and the next year he submitted his resignation. In May, 1803, after spending twenty-three years in the Upper House, his active political career ended. He did not, however, give up the post of Judge of Probate, and he did not resign his County Court position until 1805. He retained an interest in Connecticut politics and asked his son-in-law, John McClellan, in 1804, to provide him with information about the activities of the General Assembly. Now well over seventy, his health gradually declined. By July, 1810, he admitted to his son that he was exceedingly feeble and could not "walk about [the] House without a cane." The death of his favorite son Solomon in October, 1810, was a blow from which he never recovered. His health failed rapidly thereafter and death occurred on August 2, 1811.[11]

*

Any evaluation of William Williams must consider the relationship between Williams and Jonathan Trumbull, Sr. The two were close personal friends and political allies. It could be argued that Williams was Trumbull's political satellite and mouthpiece, but the evidence from the correspondence of Williams does not support this conclusion. It would be unnatural to assume that he was not influenced by the older Trumbull, but the sources of Williams' political culture came from his entire experience and upbringing. Williams absorbed the evangelical and political world view of the New Lights, a perspective that prevailed in Windham County and, far more significantly, was the world view of his father, the Reverend Solomon Williams. The attitudes Williams assimilated as a youth remained with him throughout his life. Although their political views were very similar, subtle distinctions differentiated Trumbull and Williams. Trumbull, a generation older and holding a far more sensitive political position, acted more cautiously. Unlike Williams, he did not publish fiery essays, denouncing the king and the British crown. Trumbull had a strong mercantile bias that Williams did not share. During the war, the Governor often seemed much more interested in supporting the interests and increasing the profits of his merchant friends than in paying the army or considering the sufferings of the ordinary populace. A consequence of this partiality was Trumbull's opposition to price controls and, in the 1780s, a strong nationalist persuasion. Williams, on the other hand, never believed that the Revolution was being fought to benefit profiteers, and he firmly championed price controls. He later opposed what he considered to be the selfish interests of the nationalists to gain profit at the expense of the general populace.

Many leaders of the Patriot party in Connecticut were *prima donnas,* and Williams and the Trumbulls proved no exceptions. Williams' tactlessness, credulity, and narrow-mindedness led to disagreements, while the hypersensitivity, the lust for position, and avidness for monetary reward on the part of the Trumbulls and their allies led to a disillusionment on Williams' part that lasted until the adoption of the Constitution. His disputes with Joseph and Jonathan, Jr., although serious, lasted only a short time. The relationship between Joseph Trumbull and Williams was congenial until the end of 1777, while his rift with Jonathan, Jr., was equally short. Although Trumbull and Williams stood at opposite ends of the political spectrum in the 1780s, no evidence exists that these political differences extended to the personal sphere.

Williams was an old-fashioned political type. He was deeply religious, honest, dedicated, and an ardent patriot, but he was also impetuous, tactless, parochial, inflexible, and difficut to like. The predominant source of his politics and lifestyle was religion, because he viewed all aspects of life through New Light lenses. Born and raised in the midst of the turmoils of the Great Awakening and deeply influenced by his pastor father, he retained this perspective throughout a long and active life. Chosen Deacon in 1768, he always remained active in the affairs of the First Church of Lebanon. After his father's death, he labored in vain to procure the minister's office for his nephew, Solomon Williams. His letters are replete with invocations for God's aid and requests for His blessing, particularly in time of stress, and, while in Congress, he voted in favor of a resolution to import twenty thousand copies of the Bible. His main objection to the federal Constitution was that it prohibited any religious test for office, and it is surely characteristic that from 1782 until his death he kept a journal exclusively devoted to memoranda of sermons.[12]

His tactlessness, impetuousity, and, in consequence, his knack for making enemies is exemplified by his spreading of rumors against Joseph Trumbull in 1777. Eliphalet Dyer, whose personal relationship with Williams was chilly, though they were close political allies, best summed up these traits when he stated that Trumbull should know the Colonel well enough to understand "the suddeness of his Temper, the warmth of his Imagination, the strong Impression sometimes a little matter makes on his mind (tho' of an honest good heart) to lay so great a Stress upon his painting."[13] These qualities, together with his sternness, religiosity, and a total belief in his own rightousness, won him enemies, particularly among the merchant friends of Silas Deane. Williams never trusted merchant patriots, men whose pursuit of the "main chance" seemed, in his eyes, to distort and degrade their patriotism. Williams, too, was a small inland merchant, but he never engaged in international trade and was in reality just a shopkeeper. His politics were not shaped by his career in business, and he distrusted those whose politics were.

Never once during the long struggle against Britain did he doubt the justice of the American cause or waver in his devotion to duty. Williams labored at the very center of the Revolution in Connecticut and took part in virtually all important decisions from his positions in the legislature, the Committee of Correspondence, and the Council of Safety. When he wanted to use his political muscle, a good deal of muscle existed to wield. If the friends of Silas Deane can be believed, Speaker Williams was the man most responsible for Deane's recall from Congress. Generally however, Williams worked behind the scenes, and he filled a perfect position to influence decisively events in the direction he favored.

An ardent and eloquent propagandist, he thundered opposition to the British crown and, although he by no means favored civil war, he never flinched, he never backtracked, he never hesitated. Williams' mark on national affairs was slight, but in Connecticut, William Williams, a dedicated, old-fashioned, stern, and contentious patriot, was one of the three or four pivotal figures in the independence movement.

Notes

COMMON ABBREVIATIONS

CHS   The Connecticut Historical Society
CHSC   *Collections of the Connecticut Historical Society*
CR   *Public Records of the Colony of Connecticut*
CSL   The Connecticut State Library
HSP   The Historical Society of Pennsylvania
JT   Jonathan Trumbull
JosT   Joseph Trumbull
MHSC   *Massachusetts Historical Society Collections*
NYHS   New York Historical Society
NYHSC *Collections of the New York Historical Society*
NYPL   New York Public Library
SR   *The Public Records of the State of Connecticut*
WP   Williams Papers
WW   William Williams

A LEBANON BOYHOOD AND YOUTH

1. Clifford K. Shipton, *Sibley's Harvard Graduates* (Boston, 1965), XIII, 163; Harrison Williams, *The Life Ancestors and Descendents of Robert Williams of Roxbury* (Washington, D.C., 1934), 100-105, 126-35; Solomon Williams to Elisha Williams, Mar. 10, 1750, Beinecke Library, Yale University; Solomon Williams to Eliphalet Williams, Mar. 6, 1761, Knollenberg Collection, Yale.

2. Shipton, *Harvard Graduates* (1942), VI, 352-59; Franklin Bowditch Dexter, ed,. *Itineraries and Correspondence of Ezra Stiles* (New Haven, 1916), 503; Williams, *Robert Williams*, 103.

3. Bruce P. Stark, "Lebanon, Connecticut: A Study of Society and Politics in the Eighteenth Century" (unpublished Ph.D. dissertation, The University of Connecticut, 1970), 6-20.

4. Jackson Turner Main, *The Social Structure of Revolutionary America* (Princeton, N.J., 1965), 7, 18; Albert Laverne Olsen, *Agricultural Economy and the Population in Eighteenth-Century Connecticut, [Tercentenary Pamphlet, XL]* (New Haven, 1935), 5-8.

5. Elkanah Tisdale, A Statistical Account of Lebanon in the County of Windham, MSS, 1800, CHS, 2-4.

6. Shipton, *Harvard Graduates*, VI, 140-41, 353, 381; Franklin Bowditch Dexter, *Biographical Sketches of the Graduates of Yale College* (New York, 1885), I, 252-53; Windham County Court Records, I, 1726-1732, CSL, 87; Glenn Weaver, *Jonathan Trumbull: Connecticut's Merchant Magistrate* (Hartford, 1956), 5, 12.

7. Lebanon, Connecticut, Proprietors Records, 1716-1786, Lebanon Town Records, Box 668, CHS.

8. Stark, "Lebanon," 159, 187-88, 197-99. The extent of the migration from Connecticut is alluded to by Ezra Stiles. Stiles, *Itineraries*, 50-51; Franklin Bowditch Dexter, ed., *The Literary Diary of Ezra Stiles* (New York, 1901), I, 443.

9. Williams, *Robert Williams*, 17-106 *passim; Appleton's Cyclopaedia of American Biography* (New York, 1889), VI, 523-26; [Mrs. Stephen Prime, *Genealogy of the Williams Family,*] 1-5.

10. Williams, *Robert Williams*, 64-68; Shipton, *Harvard Graduates*, V, 471-474; VI, 25-35; Dexter, *Yale Graduates*, I, 695-96; II, 69-70, 395-96.

11. Shipton, *Harvard Graduates*, V, 498-501; Williams, *Robert Williams*, 63-64, 78-79.

12. Williams, *Robert Williams*, 96-97, 106-07, 137-38; Shipton, *Harvard Graduates*, V, 588-94; Lebanon Town Records, Lebanon Town Hall, I, 64; Lebanon, Connecticut, Land Records, CSL, II, 204-05, 409-10, 483-84.

13. Williams, *Robert Williams*, 61-62, 74-75; Shipton, *Harvard Graduates*, VII, 612-23; *CR*, X, 321; XII, 609; XIII, 5-6; Lebanon Land, II, 412-14; Lebanon Records, I, 61-290, *passim;* Lebanon First Congregational Records, IV, 83.

14. Prime, *Williams*, 1-5; Williams, *Robert Williams*, 16-17; Lebanon Land, II, 299-300.

15. Williams, *Robert Williams*, 121-24; Lebanon Records, II, *passim;* Lebanon Goshen Congregational Church Records, I, 54-108, *passim.*

16. *CR*, XI, 2-3.

17. If one included connections through the female line, the correlation is even higher. For example, Eleazar Williams of Mansfield's only daughter married the Reverend Joseph Meacham of Coventry. Two of Solomon Williams' daughters also married ministers. Mary married the Reverend Richard Salter of Mansfield, the successor of Eleazar Williams, and Eunice married the Reverend Timothy Stone of Goshen Parish in Lebanon. Williams, *Robert Williams*, 79, 135.

18. Williams, *Robert Williams*, 74-75, 78-79, 106-07, 137-38.

19. Dexter, *Yale Graduates*, I, 753.

20. Dexter, *Yale Graduates*, I, 751-52; Williams, *Robert Williams*, 126, Shipton, *Harvard Graduates* (1958), X, 33; Titus Hosmer to Silas Deane, Sept. 4, 1774, *Deane Papers, CHSC* (1880), II, 155.

21. Williams, *Robert Williams*, 126-27; Silas Deane to Samuel H. Parsons, *Deane Papers, CHSC*, II, 130-31; *CR*, XII, 454; XV, 36; *SR*, I, 249.

22. Williams, *Robert Williams*, 135; Shipton, *Harvard Graduates*, X, 404-09; *Contributions to the Ecclesiastical History of Connecticut* (New Haven, 1861), 418; Dexter, *Yale Graduates* (1896), II, 439; *CR*, XII, 452, 546; XIII, 3, 169, 175, 290; *SR*, V, 316; Dexter, *Yale Graduates* (1903), III, 47-48.

23. Philogrammatical Library, Lebanon, Connecticut, CHS; Ellen D. Larned, *History of Windham County* (Worcester, Mass., 1874), I, 356; Solomon Williams to [Benjamin] Colman, Jan. 11, 1739; Thomas Cushing, Jr., to Solomon Williams, Nov., 1739, CHS.

24. Richard L. Bushman, *From Puritan to Yankee* (Cambridge, Mass., 1967), 190-91; Howard F. Vos, "The Great Awakening in Connecticut" (unpublished Ph.D. dissertation, Northwestern University, 1967), 110.

25. James P. Walsh, "The Pure Church in Eighteenth Century Connecticut" (unpublished Ph.D. dissertation, Columbia University, 1967), 55-56; Lebanon First Records, IV, 4-8; Goshen Records, II, 9; Rev. E. H. Gillett, ed., "Diary of the Rev. Jacob Eliot," *The Historical Magazine*, 2nd Ser., V, (1869), 33-35; Edwin Scott Gausted, *The Great Awakening in New England* (New York, 1957), 47; Benjamin Trumbull, *A Complete History of Connecticut* (New Haven, 1818), II, 157, 256, Shipton, *Harvard Graduates*, V, 471-74.

26. Solomon Williams, *The More Excellent Way or The Ordinary Renewing and Sanctifying Graces of the Holy Spirit* (Boston, 1742), 25-29, 36; Solomon Williams, *The Power and Efficacy of the Prayers of the People of Lord*, (Boston, 1742), 24; Perry Miller, *Jonathan Edwards* (New York, 1959), 104-05, 174; Shipton, *Harvard Graduates*, VI, 354-56.

27. John Williams, eldest son of Colonel Israel, was graduated from Harvard in 1751, the same year as William Williams. He died at Hatfield on November 7, 1751. Shipton, *Harvard Graduates*, XIII, 162.

28. Lebanon First Records, I, 39, 42, 46, 48, 57; Lebanon Records, Box 667, CHS; Lebanon Records, I, 194; Israel Williams to Solomon Williams, Nov. 29, 1748, WP, CHS. He attended the grammer school before the famous schoolmaster Nathan Tisdale, Harvard, 1749, became associated with it. Shipton, *Harvard Graduates*, XII, 490-92.

29. Solomon Williams to Elisha Williams, Mar. 10, 1749/50, Beinecke, Yale; Solomon Williams to WW, May 27, 1751, WP, CHS; Shipton, *Harvard Gradutes*, XIII, 163.

30. WW, Account Book, 1756-64; Daybook 1767-1774; "Memorandum of Goods for Wm Williams Esqr.," Jan. 9, 1764; "Shop Papers," Oct., 1764, WP, CHS; Lebanon Records, I, 210.

31. Dexter, *Yale Graduates*, I, 733; CR, V, 413, 485; CR, IV-X, *passim;* Lebanon Records, I, 3-210, *passim;* Lebanon Land, I-II, *passim.*

32. Lebanon Records, I, 210-391, *passim;* CR, XI, 1, 57, 174, 244, 250, 303, 367, 436.

33. John Sanderson, *Biography of the Signers of the Declaration of Independence* (Philadelphia, 1823), IV, 90-105; Shipton, *Harvard Graduates*, XIII, 164-66; Silas Deane to Mrs. Deane, Jan. 21, 1776, *Deane Papers, CHS*, II, 351.

34. WW, Mar. 1, 1761; WW to Joseph Trumbull, Dec. 12, 1763; WW to Miss Faith Trumble, Jan., 1765; Solomon Williams to Mrs. Elizabeth Smith, Feb. 28, 1771, WP, CHS; Shipton, *Harvard Graduates*, XIII, 166; XV (1970), 409.

35. WW to Mary Williams, Sept. 30, 1776, Jan. 17, 1778, Oct. 31, 1780, Oct. 9, 1782, May 23, 1783, May 29, 1783, Oct. 17, 1783, Oct. 29, 1784, May 12, 1787; Mary Williams to WW, Jul. 20, 1777, Jun. 10, 1781, May 21, 1783, Jun. 1, 1783, WP, CHS.

36. Williams, *Robert Williams*, 128-31; Dexter, *Yale Graduates*, (1907), IV, 425-26; (1911), V, 50-51, 174-75; WW to Mary Williams, May 23, 1783, May 21, 1789; Mary Williams to WW, May 21, 1783, Jun. 1, 1783, WP, CHS; WW to Mary Williams, May 31, 1783, J. Pierpont Morgan Library, New York.

NEW LIGHT POLITICS AND THE STAMP ACT CRISIS

1. Stark, "Lebanon," 131-36; Bushman, *Puritan to Yankee*, 235-44.

2. Bushman, *Puritan to Yankee*, 223-28, 236-60; Oscar Zeichner, *Connecticut's Years of Controversy* (Chapel Hill, N.C., 1949), 22-24; Christopher Collier, *Roger Sherman's Connecticut* (Middletown, Conn., 1971), 46; Shipton, *Harvard Graduates*, VI, 357.

3. Zeichner, *Years of Controversy*, 26; Bushman, *Puritan to Yankee*, 253; Dexter, *Yale Graduates*, II, 48-49; Daniel Lyman to WW, Sept. 3, 1759, WP, CHS.

4. CR, XI, 250, 342-43, 389-91.

5. CR, XI, 480, 487; Weaver, *Trumbull*, 86-87; Covenant, Jun. 5, 1761, WP, CHS.

6. Weaver, *Trumbull*, 87; Dexter, *Yale Graduates*, II, 216; Connecticut Archives, Colonial Wars, 1st Ser., V, 272; VI, 58, 60; VII, 179, VIII, 185, CSL; CR, X, 472; WW to JT, June 26, 1761, Jonathan Trumbull, Sr., Papers, CHS; Trumbull Papers, IV, 35, CSL.

7. Weaver, *Trumbull*, 88; WW to JT, June 26, 1761, Aug. 10, 1761, Jonathan Trumbull, Sr., Papers, CHS; Eleazar Fitch to JT, June 27, 1761, French and Indian War Papers, CHS.

8. Sanderson, *Signers*, IV, 90; WW to JT, Aug. 10, 1761, Jonathan Trumbull, Sr., Papers, CHS.

9. Zeichner, *Years of Controversy*, 20-51, *passim;* Stark, "Lebanon," 361-63.

10. Bushman, *Puritan to Yankee*, 258-65; Stark, "Lebanon," 363-64.

11. Bernard Bailyn, *The Ideological Origins of the American Revolution* (Cambridge, Mass., 1967), 33-62; Bernard Bailyn, *The Origins of American Politics* (New York, 1970), 10-14.

12. *CR*, XII, 240; Connecticut Archives, Revolutionary War, 1st. Ser., I, 8; Zeichner, *Years of Controversy*, 45-47; Edmund S. Morgan and Helen M. Morgan, *The Stamp Act Crisis* (New York, 1962), 36-37.

13. CR, XII, 256, 299-300; Lawrence Henry Gipson, *American Loyalist: Jared Ingersoll* (New Haven, 1971), 123-25; Zeichner, *Years of Controversy*, 49; Edmund S. Morgan, "Colonial Ideas of Parliamentary Power, 1764-1766," in *The Reinterpretation of the American Revolution, 1763-1789*, ed. by Jack P. Greene (New York, 1968), 157.

14. Old Light deputy, Benjamin Gale, described the evolution of the Sons of Liberty. "Several Factions wh. have subsisted in this Colony, originating with the N London Society—thence matamorphisd into the Faction for paper Emissions on Loan, thence into N. Light, into the Susquehannah and Delaware Factions,—into Orthodoxy—now into Stamp Duty." Zeichner, *Years of Controversy*, 52.

15. Others identified as leaders of the Sons were William Pitkin, Jr., Jonathan Sturgis, Thaddeus Burr, Samuel Bradley, Jr., John Brooks, Le Grand Cannon, John Burrows, Aaron Cleveland, Azel Fitch, and Samuel Huntington. Zeichner, *Years of Controversy*, 52; Pauline Maier, *From Resistance to Revolution* (New York, 1972), 304-07; Gipson, *Ingersoll*, 182, 200; Morgans, *Stamp Act*, 161-67.

16. Albert E. Van Dusen, *Connecticut* (New York, 1961), 126-27; Zeichner, *Years of Controversy*, 51-52; Maier, *Resistance*, 304-07; Morgans, *Stamp Act*, 161-67; Gipson, *Ingersoll*, 166-72.

17. *The Connecticut Courant*, Sept. 2, 1765. According to Samuel Peters, an Anglican clergyman from Hebron and an extremely unreliable source, the effigies represented Ingersoll, the Devil, and George Grenville. The Devil's clothes were appropriately provided by the Reverend Solomon Williams, Grenville's clothes by Jonathan Trumbull, and Ingersoll's by Joseph Trumbull. [Samuel Peters,] *A General History of Connecticut* (New Haven, 1829), 250-51.

18. JT to Governor Fitch, *Fitch Papers, CHSC* (Hartford, 1920), II, 353.

19. Larned, *Windham County* (1880), II, 114; Morgans, *Stamp Act*, 296; Gipson, *Ingersoll*, 177-87; *CR*, XII, 409-10.

20. WW, [1765?,] WP, CHS.

21. WW to Eleazar Wheelock, Oct. 16, 1765, The Papers of Eleazar Wheelock, Dartmouth College Library, microfilm edition, III.

22. *CR*, XII, 413, 420-25; Zeichner, *Years of Controversy*, 55-56; Morgan, "Parliamentary Power," *Reinterpretation Revolution*, 163; Stiles, *Itineraries*, 221-22.

23. The "great Chair" was the Governor, and the "4 Elbows" were the four Old Light Councillors, who stood with the Governor and took the oath to uphold the Stamp Act.

24. WW to Mr. Lyman, Dec. 25, 1765, HSP.

25. Ibid. This sentiment was echoed by other observers in late 1765. Leverett Hubbard affirmed that radicals aimed not only at burying "the Stamp act but the Gov. also." Chauncey Whittelsey emphasized that the Governor and his four friends "are threatened with Polittical Death, next Election, and I fear, some of them will be executed." Leverett Hubbard to Ezra Stiles, Nov. 6, 1765; Chauncy Whittelsey to Ezra Stiles, Dec. 24, 1765, Stiles, *Itineraries*, 512-13, 588-89.

26. Zeichner, *Years of Controversy*, 60-62; *New London Gazette*, Nov. 15, 1765.

27. Captain Azel Fitch (1728-1769) served in the French and Indian War with Hugh Ledlie and other leaders of the Sons of Liberty. Fitch was a man of reputation in Lebanon because of his service against the French. He filled twelve town and society offices, including one term as Constable and three on the Parish Committee of the First Society, CR, XI, 97, 227, 354, 486, 602, 621; Lebanon Records, I, 210-258, passim; Lebanon First Records, II, 14-22.

28. Gipson, Ingersoll, 200-02; WW to Mr. Lyman, Dec. 25, 1765, HSP.

29. Zeichner, Years of Controversy, 64, 72-73; William Floyd Willingham, "Windham, Connecticut: Profile of a Revolutionary Community, 1755-1818" (unpublished Ph.D. dissertation, Northwestern University, 1972), 109; WW to Mr. Lyman, Dec. 25, 1765; Sons of Liberty To the Sons of Liberty, Conven'd at Hartford, Mar. 24, 1766, HSP.

30. Zeichner, Years of Controversy, 73-74; Willingham, "Windham," 108-09; Connecticut Courant, Mar. 31, 1766; George Groce, William Samuel Johnson (New York, 1937), 64-66.

31. Six new Assistants were elected, four to replace defeated Old Lights, one to replace Deputy-Governor Trumbull, and one to fill a vacancy caused by the death of Old Light Daniel Edwards on September 6, 1765. CR, XII, 411.

32. The Twelfth Regiment included companies from Lebanon, Hebron, East Haddam, and Marlborough Society in Colchester, Royal R. Hinman, Historical Collection of the Part Sustained by Connecticut during the War of Revolution (Hartford, 1842), 11; CR, VIII, 278.

33. CR, XII, 414, 453, 459, 466-67; Connecticut Courant, Mar. 31, 1766; Van Dusen, Connecticut, 128; Connecticut Archives, Revolutionary War, 1st Ser., I, 36, 37, 39. Williams served temporarily as Clerk, in the absence of Pitkin, in parts of 1764 and 1765. Connecticut Archives, Revolutionary War, 1st Ser., I, 12, 29-33.

34. CR, XII, 502. The heirs of John Mason, who claimed to be the protectors of the Mohegan Indians, asserted that the colony had fraudulently acquired their tribal lands in eastern Connecticut. William Samuel Johnson was sent to London to assist Agent Richard Jackson in defending Connecticut before the Privy Council. An adverse decision in this crucial matter would have invalidated the titles for thousands of persons who lived on the disputed lands, and a verdict that the colony had illegally acquired the lands could have been used as grounds for abrogating Connecticut's charter. It is, therefore, not surprising that three of the four members of the committee, Trumbull, Williams, and Griswold, lived in the disputed region. Johnson skillfully defended Connecticut's interests, and in June, 1771, the Council upheld the position of the colony. Groce, Johnson, 89-90.

35. CR, XII, 563, 614-15; XIII, 75-76, 186, 238, 301-03, 517.

36. CR, XII, 615, 638, 640; XIII, 78-79, 189-90.

37. Ibid., XIII, 94, 129, 139, 206, 281-82, 314-15, 405, 406, 425-26, 481-82, 535-37, 599; XIV, 24, 44, 106, 170-71, 211.

THE COMING OF THE REVOLUTION

1. Morgan, "Parliamentary Power," Reinterpretation Revolution, 165-79; CR, XII, 423-24; Edmund S. Morgan, The Birth of the Republic (Chicago, 1956), 31-34; Robert J. Claffin, "The Townshend Acts of 1767," The William and Mary Quarterly, Third Series, XXVII (1970), 90-119, passim.

2. Lawrence Henry Gipson, The Coming of the Revolution (New York, 1954), 174, 181; Larned, Windham County, II, 115-18; Lebanon Records, I, 264-65.

3. Morgan, Birth, 35; Gazette, Apr. 29, 1768; Connecticut Courant, May 9, 1768.

4. Zeichner, *Years of Controversy*, 83-85; *CR*, XIII, 72-74, 84-90.

5. Oliver M. Dickerson, *The Navigation Acts and the American Revolution* (New York, 1963), 208, 236-38; Hiller B. Zobel, *The Boston Massacre* (New York, 1970), 65-110, *passim*.

6. JT to William Samuel Johnson, Jul. 4, 1768, William Samuel Johnson Papers, CHS; Solomon Williams to Mrs. Elizabeth Smith, Jun. 28, 1768, Beinecke, Yale.

7. WW to William Samuel Johnson, Jul. 5, 1768, William Samuel Johnson Papers, CHS.

8. *Gazette*, Sept. 30, 1768.

9. WW to William Samuel Johnson, Jul. 24, 1769, William Samuel Johnson Papers, CHS.

10. *CR*, XIII, 236; WW to Nathaniel Wales and Samuel Gray, Jan. 29, 1770. WP, CHS.

11. Morgan, *Birth*, 47-48; Zobel, *Massacre*, 180-205.

12. Orlo D. Hine, *Early Lebanon* (Hartford, 1880), 27-29; Lebanon Town Records, Box 668, CHS.

13. Zeichner, *Years of Controversy*, 86-88; Morgan, *Birth*, 50; Larned, *Windham County*, II, 118; Lebanon Town Records, Box 668, CHS.

14. Lebanon Town Records, Box 668, CHS; Hine, *Early*, 30-31; Larned, *Windham County*, II, 120.

15. Zeichner, *Years of Controversy*, 113-18, *CR*, XIII, 236; John Devotion to Ezra Stiles, Apr. 22, 1767, June 6, 1767, Stiles, *Itineraries*, 462-66.

16. Zeichner, *Years of Controversy*, 121-25; WW to William Samuel Johnson, Jul. 24, 1769, William Samuel Johnson Papers, CHS.

17. Connecticut Secretary of State Statistics, CHS.

18. The two most recent studies on Susquehannah are Willingham, "Windham," and Richard Thomas Warfle, "Connecticut's Critical Period: The Response to the Susquehannah Affair, 1769-1774" (unpublished Ph.D. dissertation, The University of Connecticut, 1972).

19. Julian P. Boyd, *The Susquehannah Company: Connecticut's Experiment in Expansion*, [*Tercentenary Pamphlet*, XXXIV] (New Haven, 1935) 5-36; Van Dusen, *Connecticut*, 124, 128-29.

20. Zeichner, *Years of Controversy*, 107; WW to William Samuel Johnson, Jul. 24, 1769, William Samuel Johnson Papers, CHS.

21. Warfle, "Susquehannah Affair," 1-3, 137-43; *CR*, XIV, 160-61; Collier, *Sherman*, 78.

22. Dyer evidently believed that Williams had doublecrossed him, and this was the source of Dyer's dislike of Williams. He believed, wrongly, said Williams, that Williams had "set You up some years since for ye second Chair & then sacrifice[d] You to another." Although they maintained a political alliance, relations between the two always remained cool. WW to Eliphalet Dyer, Nov. 26, 1773, NYHS.

23. Warfle, "Susquehannah Affair," 144-51; *CR*, XIV, 217-18.

24. Zeichner, *Years of Controversy*, 155-58, 194.

25. *CR*, XIII, 175, 581; XIV, 253, 256, 327, 384; XV, 7, 43, 146, 173-74, 272; Peter Force ed., *American Archives* (Washington, D.C., 1839), 4th Series, II, 706.

26. At least five members of the Committee of Correspondence had connections with Susquehannah: Parsons, Deane, Wales, Trumbull, and Williams. Zeichner, *Years of Controversy*, 137-141; *CR*, XIV, 156, 161.

27. Richard D. Brown, *Revolutionary Politics in Massachusetts* (Cambridge, Mass., 1970), 38-57, 123-24, 140-41; Zeichner, *Years of Controversy*, 138-41; *CR*, XIV, 156, 161; Connecticut Committee of Correspondence to the Virginia Com-

mittee, Aug. 10, 1773, NYPL. In all documents relating to the Committee of Correspondence, Williams is listed second, after Ebenezer Silliman, indicating that he was considered the second most prominent member. *CR*, XIV, 156; Connecticut Archives, Revolutionary War, 1st Ser., I, 54-56.

28. Morgan, *Birth*, 49-51; WW and others to the Virginia House of Burgesses, Mar. 8, 1774, Sparks, 71, Harvard College Library.

29. *CR*, XIV, 261, 324, 347-50; Committee of Correspondence for Connecticut to the Committee of Correspandence at Boston, Force, *American Archives*, (1837), I, 304-05; *Collections of the Massachusetts Historical Society* (Boston, 1858), XXXIV, 16-17.

30. Zeichner, *Years of Controversy*, 162-64; Larned, *Windham County*, II, 121-28.

31. Hine, *Early*, 32-33; *Gazette*, June 3, 1774. The *New London Gazette* changed its name in December, 1773, to *The Connecticut Gazette and Universal Intelligencer*.

32. *Gazette*, Jul. 1, 1774; Jul. 30, 1774; WP, CHS.

33. *Gazette*, Jul. 8, 1774; "Cato Americanus," WP, CHS.

34. *Gazette*, Jul. 29, 1774; Lebanon Town Records, Box 668, CHS.

35. Jonathan Trumbull, Jr., to Dr. Joseph Warren, June 3, 1774, Henrietta W. Hubbard Collection, CSL, 109; Selectmen of Lebanon to Selectmen of Boston, Aug. 8, 1774; WW to Dr. Joseph Warren, Oct. 3, 1774, *MHSC*, XXXIV, 42-45, 96-97.

36. Williams and Deane detested one another. Williams' patriotism was deep-seated and founded on religious conviction. He inherited the religious and political beliefs of the New Lights, and never swerved from a total adherence and devotion to the American cause. He distrusted merchants like Deane, whose patriotism was tranished by an equal devotion to private interest. Deane responded in kind. He considered Williams "a little malevolent prig in buckram" and blamed him for his recall from Congress in October, 1775. Collier, *Sherman*, 130-36; WW to Samuel Adams, Jul. 30, 1774, Samuel Adams Papers, NYPL; Silas Deane to Mrs. Deane, Oct. 2, 1775, Jan. 21, 1776, Mar. 1, 1776, *Deane Papers*, CHSC, II, 310, 351, 361; John Trumbull to Silas Deane, Oct. 20, 1775; Silas Deane to Mrs. Deane, Dec. 15, 1775; Thomas Mumford to Silas Deane, Jan. 10, 1776, *Deane Papers, Collections of the New York Historical Society* (New York, 1886, 1890), I, 87, 95; V, 551.

37. Silas Deane, along with Williams, was one of several persons chosen to take care of the correspondence of the organization. Thereafter, Deane no longer signed Committee of Correspondence documents.

38. WW to Samuel Adams, Jul. 30, 1774, Samuel Adams Papers, NYPL.

39. The leaders of the patriots included Seth Wright, Asahel Clark, Joseph Hill, and David Trumbull of Lebanon and Timothy Larrabee, Hezekiah Huntington, Vine Elderkin, Ebenezer Gray, and John Ripley of Windham. [Peters,] *General History* (1829), 298-99; [Samuel Peters,] *A General History of Connecticut* (New York, 1877), 262-69; Trumbull Papers, CSL, IV, 39.

40. Willingham, "Windham," 132-36; Larned, *Windham County*, II, 134-35; Zeichner, *Years of Controversy*, 175; *Gazette*, Aug. 15, 1774; Nov. 11, 1774.

41. Larned, *Windham County*, II, 131-32; Hinman, *Historical Collection*, 19-20; Brown, *Revolutionary Politics*, 226.

42. Trumbull Papers, CSL, XIII, 43; Memorial to the General Assembly, Sept. 8, 1774, *Huntington Papers*, CHSC (Hartford, 1922), XX, 215-17; To the Connecticut Delegates in Congress, Sept. 8, 1774, *Deane Papers, CHSC*, II, 157-61.

43. *CR*, XIV, 327-28; WW to Thomas Williams, Oct. 19, 1774; Letters to Brother Thomas, CSL.

44. Zeichner, *Years of Controversy*, 180-81; *Gazette*, Dec. 30, 1774; Lebanon Town Records, Box 668, CHS; WW to Samuel Adams, Jan. 10, 1775, WP, CHS.

45. *Gazette*, Mar. 3, 1775.

46. Zeichner, *Years of Controversy*, 185-86; Willingham, "Windham," 142-44; Nathaniel Wales, Jr., to WW, Feb. 4, 1775, WP, CHS; WW, Speaker, to Speaker of the House of Assembly, Jamaica, Mar. 14, 1775, Force, *American Archives*, 4th Ser., II, 107-08; *CR*, XIV, 409-10.

47. Zeichner, *Years of Controversy*, 188-89; "To the Friends of American Liberty," *Gazette*, Mar. 17, 1775, WP, CHS; Letter from a Gentlemen in Connecticut, Mar. 29, 1775, Force, *American Archives*, 4th Ser., II, 113.

48. "Amicus Patriae," *Gazette*, Mar. 17, 1775, WP, CHS; "Americanus," *Gazette*, Apr. 7, 1775; WW to Col. Jedidiah Huntington, Apr. 6, 1775, HSP.

49. Connecticut Committee of Correspondence to John Hancock, Apr. 21, 1775, Force, *American Archives*, 4th Ser., II, 372-73; WW to the Selectmen of Lebanon, Apr. 27, 1775, HSP.

50. *CR*, XIV, 417-19, 430-35; Van Dusen, *Connecticut*, 134.

51. Connecticut Archives, Revolutionary War, 1st Ser., I, 119.

52. Van Dusen, *Connecticut*, 134-35; Zeichner, *Years of Controversy*, 192-94, 334; *CR*, XIV, 440-44; Jedediah Huntington to Jabez Huntington, May 2, 1775, *Huntington Papers*, *CHSC*, XX, 219-20; Collier, *Sherman*, 106; Groce, *Johnson*, 102-04. Collier argues that Williams wavered and attempted to halt the sending of Connecticut troops to Massachusetts. He is in error. His evidence is based on a letter from Samuel Holden Parsons to Joseph Trumbull, but the "Col. W" referred to is not Colonel William Williams, but Colonel Erastus Wolcott, "the Ambassador." Collier, *Sherman*, 106; Samuel H. Parsons to Joseph Trumbull, June 2, 1775, Joseph Trumbull Papers, CHS.

53. WW to JosT, May 1, 1775; WW to Joseph Warren, May 4, 1775; WW to JosT, May 6, 1775, Governor Joseph Trumbull Collection, CSL, 555, 556, 557.

54. Thomas Mumford to Silas Deane, May 14, 1775, *Deane Papers*, *CHSC*, II, 230; Zeichner, *Years of Controversy*, 194-97; Van Dusen, *Connecticut*, 137.

55. *CR*, XIV, 422; XV, 7, 17-18, 39, 43; Colonel Spencer to the Assembly of Connecticut, May 25, 1775, Force, *American Archives*, 4th Ser., II, 706. Williams resigned as Colonel of the Twelfth Regiment in December, 1776, due to the obligations of his other offices. Shipton, *Harvard Graduates*, XIII, 171.

56. WW to Thomas Williams, May 16, 1775, Letters to Brother Thomas, CSL.

57. Eight years service: Eliphalet Dyer (Windham), Nathaniel Wales, Jr. (Windham), William Hillhouse (New London); seven years: William Pitkin (Hartford), Abraham Davenport (Stamford); six years: Joseph Spencer (East Haddam), Joseph Platt Cook (Danbury); five years: Benjamin Payne (Hartford); four years: James Wadsworth (Durham), Roger Sherman (New Haven), Jedidiah Elderkin (Windham), Jedidiah Strong (Litchfield), Oliver Wolcott (Litchfield).

58. Titus Hosmer to Silas Deane, May 22, 1775, May 28, 1775, *Deane Papers*, *CHSC*, 239, 243; *CR*, XV *passim*; *SR*, I-V, *passim*.

59. *CR*, XV, 84; *SR*, III, 225, 443, 486; IV, 335.

60. *CR*, XV, 315; Van Dusen, *Connecticut*, 138; Roger Sherman to WW, Jul. 28, 1775, Edmund C. Burnett, ed., *Letters of the Members of the Continental Congress* (Washington, D.C., 1921), I, 179.

61. *CR*, XV, 107, 109-10, 125-26, 140-41, 248, 251, 253-54; WW, Diary of Two Trips to Philadelphia; John Lawrence, Treasurer, Oct., 1775, to Apr., 1776, WP, CHS.

62. Van Dusen, *Connecticut*, 138; WW to Metcalf Bowler, Jul. 12, 1775, Gertrude Selwyn Kimball, ed., *The Correspondence of the Colonial Governors of Rhode Island* (Boston, 1903), II, 441-44.

63. *CR*, XV, 146, 173-174; Hinman, *Historical Collection*, 189-90.

64. Stiles, *Literary Diary*, I, 654; John Trumbull to Silas Deane, Oct. 20, 1775; Silas Deane to Mrs. Deane, Dec. 15, 1775, *Deane Papers*, NYHSC, I, 86-87, 95; Thomas Mumford to Silas Deane, Dec. 21, 1775; Silas Deane to Mrs. Deane, Jan. 21, 1776; *Deane Papers*, CHSC, 345, 349-51; Thomas Mumford to Silas Deane, Jan. 10, 1776, *Deane Papers*, NYHSC (1890), V, 551; Rupert Charles Loucks, "Connecticut in the American Revolution," (master's thesis, University of Wisconsin, 1959), 129-30; Willingham, "Windham," 148-50.

65. Van Dusen, *Connecticut*, 143; WW to Thomas Williams, Dec. 27, 1775, Letters to Brother Thomas, CSL.

66. A story that is apocryphal in nature, but true in its spirit, exemplified Williams' zeal. Towards the end of 1776, when patriot fortunes appeared especially grim, Williams had a conversation with Council members William Hillhouse and Benjamin Huntington. The talk turned to the dangers which would come should Britain be victorious. Williams remarked that he would probably be hanged because of his exertions on behalf of liberty and because he had signed the Declaration of Independence. The other two had no such fears. Hillhouse averred that he would endeavor to act in a proper manner, and Huntington asserted that since he had signed neither the Declaration nor anything else in opposition to the British crown, he was safe from the gallows. Williams replied, "then, sir, you ought to be hanged for not doing your duty." Sanderson, *Signers*, IV, 100-01.

67. WW to Ezekiel Williams, Feb. 12, 1776, Beinecke, Yale; WW to Whom it may Concern, Mar. 15, 1776, WP, CHS; Shipton, *Harvard Graduates*, XIII, 167; Sanderson, *Signers*, IV, 95-101.

68. Collier, *Sherman*, 126; Van Dusen, *Connecticut*, 139-40; *CR*, XV, 281, 398-400; Connecticut Archives, Revolutionary War, 1st Ser., IV, 68; WW to JosT, May 20, 1776, Governor Joseph Trumbull Collection, CSL, 559.

69. Loucks claimed that Williams' popularity fluctuated violently during the war, and he established this view from a misinterpretation of the nominations lists. In the fall nominations, incumbents were listed strictly in order of seniority, and only non-Assistants by popularity. The only exception to this generalization appears to be in October, 1776. Whether by clerical error, design, or popular vote, Signers Oliver Wolcott and Samuel Huntington were listed third and fourth, Williams twelfth, and the senior Assistants, Hamlin and Sheldon, thirteenth and fourteenth. The placing of William Williams varied only as he became "more senior." If an incumbent were defeated for re-election and was nominated the next fall, however, he was placed ahead of all other non-incumbents, regardless of his total vote. Hence, when Joseph Spencer failed to gain re-election in May, 1778, he was placed fifteenth on the nominations list in October, 1778, behind the Governor, Deputy-Governor, and the twelve Assistants. Williams' position on the nominations list was precisely the same. He ranked fourteenth in 1777, thirteenth in 1778, fifteenth in 1782, and eleventh in 1783. Loucks, "Connecticut," 129; *SR*, I, 39, 221, 447; II, 3, 160, 251; V, 80, 109, 313.

70. WW to JosT, Jun. 15, 1776, Gov. Joseph Trumbull Collection, CSL, 560; "Original Draft of Proclamation for Reformation," Jun. 18, 1776, Jonathan Trumbull, Sr., Papers, CHS; Van Dusen, *Connecticut*, 140; *CR*, 415-22, 450-53.

71. Connecticut Archives, Revolutionary War, 1st Ser., I, 267, 269; IV, 25, 28b, 34, 55, 56, 63, 68, 71, 72, 83, 95, 170, 298, 299, 302, 306; "A Friend to His Country," WP, CHS.

72. WW to William Samuel Johnson, Jul. 5, 1768, William Samuel Johnson Papers, CHS; *Connecticut Courant*, May 9, 1768; "America," *Gazette*, Jul. 1, 1774; *Gazette*, Jul. 29, 1774.

73. *Gazette*, June 3, 1774; "Cato Americanus," *Gazette*, Jul. 8, 1774; "A Friend to His Country," WP, CHS; WW to JosT, May 1, 1775, Gov. Joseph Trumbull Collection, CSL, 555; WW to Metcalf Bowler, Kimball, *Correspondence Governors Rhole Island*, II, 442; WW to Selectmen of Lebanon, Apr. 27, 1775, HSP; *Gazette*, Jul. 29, 1774.

74. WW to Nathaniel Wales and Samuel Gray, Jan. 29, 1770, WP, CHS; "Cato Americanus," *Gazette*, Jul. 8, 1774; *Gazette*, Dec. 30, 1774; Hine, *Early*, 27; *Gazette*, Jun. 3, 1774; Jul. 8, 1774; Jul. 29, 1774; "Americus Patriae," WP, CHS.

75. "A Friend to His Country," WP, CHS.

THE YEARS OF WAR

1. Larry R. Gerlach, "A Delegation of Steady Habits," *The Connecticut Historical Society Bulletin*, XXXII (1967), 36-37.

2. *CR*, XV, 475-76; Burnett, *Letters Congress* (1923), II, xl; WW to J[abe]z Huntington, Aug. 12, 1776, New Haven Colony Historical Society; WW to Mary Williams, Sept. 30, 1776, WP, CHS; Oliver Wolcott to Mrs. Wolcott, Nov. 24, 1776, Burnett, *Letters Congress*, II, 163-64; *Journals of Congress* (New York, [n.d.]) III, 252, 555; *SR*, V, 207, 318.

3. WW to JT, Sept. 20, 1776, Force, *American Archives*, 5th Ser. (1851), II, 408-10. See aslo WW to Mary Williams, Sept. 30, 1776, WP, CHS; WW to JT, Jul. 5, 1777, *Historical Magazine*, New Series, IV, 223-24; WW to JT, Aug. 26, 1777, Sept. 13, 1777, *Trumbull Papers, MHSC* (1902), XXXIV, 135, 140.

4. Edmund C. Burnett, *The Continental Congress* (New York, 1941), 242-43; WW to J[abe]z Huntington, Aug. 12, 1776, New Haven Colony Historical Society; W W to JT, Jul. 5, 1777, *Hist. Magazine*, New Series, IV, 224.

5. WW to J[abe]z Huntington, Aug. 12, 1776, NHCHS; WW to JT, Jul. 5, 1777, *Hist. Magazine*, New Series, IV, 224; WW to JT, Aug. 26, 1777, Sept. 13, 1777, Trumbull Papers, *MHSC*, XXIV, 134, 142.

6. WW to JosT, Aug. 7, 1776, Oct. 7, 1776, Sept. 26, 1776; WW to JT, Aug. 6, 1777, Burnett, *Letters Congress*, II, 41-42, 104, 118, 440-41.

7. Loucks, "Connecticut," 93-94, 97-98; Stark, "Lebanon," 422; *Journals of Congress* (Philadelphia, 1777), II, 352; III, 316; WW to JosT, Aug. 7, 1776, Sept. 7, 1776, Sept. 13, 1776, Oct. 7, 1776, Nov. 4, 1777, Nov. 28, 1777; Eliphalet Dyer to JosT, Dec. 8, 1777, Dec. 15, 1777, Burnett, *Letters Congress*, II, 40, 78, 85, 117-18, 543, 584-85, 588.

8. WW to JosT, Aug. 10, 1776, Aug. 20, 1776, Burnett, *Letters Congress*, II, 46, 57-58.

9. Collier, *Sherman*, 135-36; Burnett, *Continental Congress*, 242-43; WW to JT, Jul. 5, 1777, *Hist. Magazine*, New Ser., IV, 224; Roger Sherman to WW, Aug. 18, 1777, Roger Sherman Correspondence, copy CSL; WW to JosT, Nov. 28, 1777, Burnett, *Letters Congress*, II, 574.

10. *Journals of Congress*, II, 330-31, 387-88, 395; III, 441.

11. Burnett, *Continental Congress*, 219-29; WW to JosT, Aug. 7, 1776, WW to Oliver Wolcott, Aug. 12, 1776, Burnett, *Letters Congress*, II, 41, 48.

12. Burnett, *Continental Congress*, 199-204; WW to JosT, Sept. 7, 1776; Sept. 13, 1776, Burnett, *Letters Congress*, II, 77-78, 85-86.

13. Burnett, *Continental Congress*, 206-10; WW to JosT, Sept. 26, 1776, Oct. 7, 1776, Oct. 10, 1776; WW to Jonathan Trumbull, Jr., Nov. 6, 1776, Burnett, *Letters Congress*, II, 103-05, 117-19, 121-22, 142.

14. WW to JT, Jul. 5, 1777, *Hist. Magazine*, New Ser., IV, 224.

15. Willard M. Wallace, *Appeal to Arms* (Chicago, 1964), 135-43; Eliphalet Dyer, Richard Law, and WW to JT, Aug. 25, 1777; WW to JT, Aug. 26, 1777, *Trumbull Papers, MHSC,* XXXIV, 131-35.

16. Burnett, *Continental Congress,* 259-60; WW to JT, Sept. 13, 1777, *Trumbull Papers, MHSC,* XXXIV, 140-43; *Journals of Congress,* III, 399-401; WW to JT, Sept. 17, 1777, Sept. 30, 1777, Burnett, *Letters Congress,* II 496, 505; WW to JT, Oct. 23, 1777, NYHS.

17. Burnett, *Continental Congress,* 237-41, 248-56; Larry R. Gerlach, "Toward 'a more perfect Union,' Connecticut, the Continental Congress, and the Constitutional Convention," *The Connecticut Historical Society Bulletin,* XXXIV (1969), 66-67; *Journals of Congress,* III, 416-19, 431-32, 436-37; WW to JT, Oct. 4, 1777, Burnett, *Letters Congress,* II, 517; Collier, *Sherman,* 159-60.

18. Stark, "Lebanon," 437-39; Extracts from Lebanon Revolutionary War Records, 15-17, CSL; WW to Samuel Adams, Feb. 9, 1778, Samuel Adams Papers, NYPL; Collier, *Sherman,* 159.

19. Collier, *Sherman,* 166-69; Gerlach, "Toward 'a more perfect Union,'" *CHSB,* XXXIV, 68; Roger Sherman to WW, Aug. 18, 1777, Sparks 49, Harvard College Library; Roger Sherman to WW, Sept. 22, 1777, WP, CHS; WW to Jabez Huntington, Oct. 22, 1777, Burnett, *Letters Congress,* II, 529.

20. Philip H. Jordan, Jr., "Connecticut Politics During the Revolution and Confederation, 1776-1789," (unpublished Ph.D. dissertation, Yale University, 1962), 106-09; Van Dusen, *Connecticut,* 161, 165; Extracts Lebanon War, CSL, 8-9.

21. Collier, *Sherman,* 136, 179-83; *SR,* I, 524-28; WW to Jonathan Trumbull, Jr., Apr. 15, 1778, WP, CHS.

22. Collier, *Sherman,* 177-78; *SR,* II, 12-13, 134.

23. Collier, *Sherman,* 178; Van Dusen, *Connecticut,* 161; Stark, "Lebanon," 441-43; *Gazette,* Jul. 28, 1779; Extracts Lebanon War, CSL, 21-23; *Connecticut Journal* (New Haven), Sept. 22, 1779.

24. Jordan, "Connecticut Politics," 109-11; Collier, *Sherman,* 179-90; WW to JT, Mar. 29, 1780, Jonathan Trumbull, Sr., Papers, CSL, XI, 122; *SR,* III, 5.

25. *SR,* III, 170, 179, 237-38, 316-17, 370, 519; IV, 133, 287; V, 109, 204, 317.

26. *SR,* I, 57-58, 161, 183; Selectmen of Lebanon to Citizens of Leb. [1777,] Medical Library, Yale; JT to Jabez Huntington, Feb. 11, 1777, Knollenberg Collection, Add. 3, Yale; WW to Keeper of Windham County Gaol, Aug. 17, 1778, WP, CHS; Loucks, "Connecticut," 120-22.

27. *SR,* I, 194; Extracts Lebanon War, CSL, 6-7, 13, 20, 24, 37; Stark, "Lebanon," 423-25.

28. Stark, "Lebanon," 425-26; *SR,* I, 396; II, 408-10; Extracts Lebanon War, CSL, 11-12, 20, 24, 30, 34, 37, 39, 42-43.

29. Stark, "Lebanon," 427-29; Extracts Lebanon War, CSL, 9, 28-32, 36, 40-41, 44-49; *SR,* II, 280-81; III, 29-30; IV, 14.

30. Rowland Ricketts, Jr., "The French in Lebanon, 1780-1781," *The Connecticut Historical Society Bulletin,* XXXVI (1971), 23-31; Allan Forbes, *France and New England* (Boston, 1927), II, 98-103; Isaac W. Stuart, *Life of Jonathan Trumbull* (Boston, 1859), 497-99, 537-38; *SR,* III, 187; WW to Mary Williams, Oct. 31, 1780, WP, CHS; Samuel Gray to Mrs. Williams, Nov. 23, 1780; Col. Dillon to Col. Williams, Nov. 23, 1780, Sterling, Yale.

31. Duc de Lauzun to WW, Feb. 26, 1781; [WW] to Duke de Lauzun, Mar. 13, 1781; Mary Williams to WW, June 10, 1781, WP, CHS; Duke de Lauzun to WW, Mar. 15, 1781, Sterling, Yale.

32. Shipton, *Harvard Graduates*, XIII, 171; Stuart, *Trumbull*, 542; Sanderson, *Signers*, IV, 92-93; Van Dusen, *Connecticut*, 168-69; WW to JT, Sept. 6, 1781, Sept. 7, 1781, WP, CHS.

THE FINAL YEARS

1. Jordan, "Connecticut Politics," 138-39; Extracts Lebanon War, CSL, 50; Instructions to Colo Wm Williams & Cap. Danl Tilden, 1782, WP, CHS.

2. WW, Sept., 2, 1782, WP, CHS.

3. Jordan, "Connecticut Politics," 132, 146-50; *Gazette*, May 2, 1783.

4. Collier, *Sherman*, 215-19; Jordan, "Connecticut Politics," 157-85, 215-20; SR, V, 109, 313, 317; WW to Mary Williams, Oct. 17, 1783, WP, CHS; *Gazette* April 9, 1784.

5. The two other new Councillors were equally favorably placed. Joseph Platt Cook ranked twelfth and Stephen Mix Mitchell fourteenth. SR, V, 317.

6. Jordan, "Connecticut Politics," 185-86.

7. Ibid., 187-90, 251-68; Shipton, *Harvard Graduates*, XIII, 171-72; *Gazette*, Dec. 29, 1786.

8. Jedediah Huntington to Andrew Huntington, May, 1787, *Huntington Papers, CHSC*, XX, 471; WW to Mary Williams, May 12, 1787, WP, CHS.

9. Jordan, "Connecticut Politics," 323; Lebanon Records, I, 361-62, 365; Shipton, *Harvard Graduates*, XIII, 173; Forrest McDonald, *We the People* (Madison, Wisc., 1958), 142; WW to Benjamin Huntington, Jan. 4, 1787, NYPL.

10. Town of Lebanon to U. S. Congress, May 1, 1796; James Hillhouse to WW, May 7, 1796, WP, CHS; SR, VIII, 360, 435; IX, 83, 158, 324, 400, X, 6-7; Shipton, *Harvard Graduates*, XIII, 173.

11. Shipton, *Harvard Graduates*, XIII, 173-74; SR, X, 106-07, 187; Joseph P. Cook to WW, May 27, 1803; WW to John McClellan, May 13, 1805, WP, CHS; WW to John McClellan, Oct. 9, 1804, Boston Public Library; WW to Solomon Williams, Jul. 1810, WP, CHS.

12. *Journals of Congress*, III, 387; Journal 1782-1811, WP, CHS.

13. Eliphalet Dyer to JosT, Dec. 15, 1777, Burnett, *Letters Congress*, II, 588.

Made in the USA
Columbia, SC
21 June 2020